366 Questions and Answers

Illustrated by Daniel Conci

ENGLAND LE8 0HG

© 1992 Happy Books, Milan
ISBN: 978-0-7097-2227-4
© 2015 Brown Watson, LE8 0HG, English edition
Printed in China

THE EARTH

One Day in Pompeii

One Day in Pompeii

THE HEAT was almost suffocating, the narrow roads of the city crowded with people going about their business, carts loaded with goods, children running around.

It was only nine o'clock in the morning – so who knew what it would be like at noon, with the sun at its height.

Despite the heat, a man in a short tunic moved quickly through the crowds. Tall and strong, drops of perspiration glistened on his dark hair and short beard, his eyes darting anxiously first one way, then the other.

Crossing the square, he became aware of a man in front of a small crowd, shouting something about the city having the signs of an earthquake, the same as had happened seventeen years before.

But nobody paid much attention. Certainly the man did not stop to listen, continuing to thread his way through the crowds, still looking all around.

Only when he reached the sports ground in the heart of the city did he pause for breath.

Suddenly, he turned his head in the direction of voices – voices from two groups of boys shouting to each other.

"There's Rufus!" the man murmured with a sigh of relief. "I have found him, at last!"

The boys had already started on a game as the man came up and laid a hand on the boy's shoulder.

"You must come with me, Rufus!" he said. "We are going to your grandparents at Nocera! We are all going to meet them at the port, near the tombstones!"

But Rufus was too involved in the game to listen. He was not at all pleased when the man seized him by the shoulder, forcing him to turn round.

"Look," he burst out, "don't give me orders, you—" He was about to say "slave". But he knew that if he dared insult Licio, the slave his father trusted so much, he would be punished.

And when he saw the anxiety and fear in Licio's eyes, his anger faded.

"All right," he said, putting on his tunic. "I'll come."

"What's wrong?" continued Rufus, following Licio as he led the way.

January

"I'm worried, Rufus. Worried – and very afraid. Since yesterday, the animals have almost gone wild, some have even tried to escape. I'm afraid of some disaster – like that time the earth moved. So, I spoke to your father, and he decided that we should go to the country for a while away from the city. He asked me to find you, whilst he went to get a pair of wagons for your mother and sister. We are due to meet them at the port of Nocera, by the tombstones!"

The two walked quickly in the humid air. Rufus wanted to tell him that it was all imagination, that the animals were only restless because of the heat. It was August, after all...

At last, they reached Nocera, thankful for a rest in the shade of an oak tree.

They did not have long to wait before two wagons carrying Rufus' family and some servants loaded with bags and pitchers came rumbling towards them. His father got down first.

"Let us rest here a while," he said. "We are tired, and there is still some way to go."

They sat in silence for some while among the tombstones under the trees, Rufus watching Licio as he went to comfort the horses. They were rolling their eyes and stamping their hooves, afraid and nervous.

"What's wrong?" asked Rufus. "What is upsetting them?"

At that moment, a cry came from a group of people nearby, pointing to the mountain which dominated the city of Pompeii. A gigantic black cloud was rising up to the sky, spreading out until it completely covered the sun. Rufus could hear people screaming as clouds of ash then cinders began rushing down, towards the city.

"It's Vesuvius!" breathed Rufus' father. "Vesuvius has awoken...."

"Everyone into the wagons!" cried Licio, jolting them back to their senses."There is no time to lose!"

Licio and Rufus' father had to pull the horses along by their reins because they refused to budge. And even as the wheels turned, they all looked back over their shoulders in horror, wondering what would become of the beautiful city of Pompeii....

1 What is a volcano?

In the depths of the Earth, the temperature is very high. Rocky substances there collect in huge underground "fireplaces", spreading out and rising up through cracks in the Earth, like natural chimneys, until they come out together through an opening in the Earth's crust to form a volcano.

An eruption happens when the hot materials continue to burn, rising up the length of the "chimneys" and exploding through the surface.

2 How do we measure an earthquake?

Sometimes the earth shakes. It may be a light tremor. Or it can shake with violence, causing a disaster.

Earth tremors are caused by continued movements of the Earth which happen at great depths.

Each of these movements is called a "seismic tremor" – like the waves around a pebble thrown into a pond.

If we think of that pebble, the point at which it falls would be the deepest point at which a tremor happens.

This is called the "epicentre", where the force of the earthquake would be at its maximum.

The further away from the epicentre, the weaker the seismic waves become.

The intensity of an earthquake is measured on the Richter Scale of 0 – 10.

At 10 on the scale, the earthquake is classed as a major disaster, with few survivors, destruction of buildings and devastation of land.

3 What is "the fire belt?"

The Earth's crust is formed by enormous layers. Between one layer and another, there is a space which makes a clearing for the hot materials coming from the depths of the Earth.

That is why, along these breaks in the Earth's crust, we find many volcanoes.

All around the Pacific Ocean, there are a series of breaks, and therefore a series of volcanoes – so many that it is called "The Belt of Fire".

4 How is the Earth made up?

If we could cut it in half, we would find the Earth is rather like an onion, with various layers around a central core.

This core, the nucleus, has a radius of 3,500 kilometres.

Around the nucleus is the "mantle", 100 kilometres thick, then the Earth's crust on which we live.

The various layers are composed of different materials, the temperature increasing the nearer they are to the nucleus.

5 What is the force of gravity?

An ice cream slips from the baby's hand to the ground. His father knocks a vase, which crashes to the floor. And a little girl cries when she falls off her bicycle.

The ice cream, the vase and the little girl have all experienced the force of gravity – the power of the earth to attract all things – objects, people, animals – towards its own surface with a force which we call "the force of gravity".

The force with which a thing is drawn towards the Earth is called "weight". If something weighs 50 kilogrammes, it will be attracted towards the Earth with a force equal to 50 kilogrammes. So, the lighter somebody is, the easier it is for them to lift themselves from the Earth's surface – in jumping, for example – because the force of gravity is less.

This is why it is easier to lift a chair, which has a small "mass" or solid body, and little weight, than, say, a refrigerator, with a much bigger mass and more weight.

6 How big is the Earth?

The Earth is slightly flat at the North and South Poles. So its measurement around the equator is 40,076,594 metres, whereas, verically around the Meridian line of longitude, it is 40,009,152. Its surface covers 510,100,000 square kilometres - 149,400,000 land and 360,700.000 oceans. The distance from the Earth to the Sun is 149,509,000 kilometres, whereas between the Earth and the Moon it is "only" 384,365 kilometres.

7 How do we get the seasons?

The Earth goes around the sun on a journey called an "orbit" once a year. Going on its orbit, Earth is slightly tilted, which means the rays of the sun hit it at different angles, bringing changes in climate four times a year – the seasons.

The angles of the rays of the sun are shortest between the two tropics of Cancer and Capricorn, and increase gradually towards the North and South Poles. This is why in tropical regions the changes in seasons are hardly noticeable, whereas, as we go towards the Poles, they become more marked.

Twice a year, the day and the night are the same length. This is an equinox. Also twice a year, the difference in duration between the day and the night is at its maximum. These are the solstices.

The 21st March is an equinox. It is the beginning of Spring in the Northern Hemisphere – the Autumn in the Southern Hemisphere! The days begin to get longer – until 22nd June, the summer solstice, when the days begin getting shorter. For 93 days, it is summer in the Northern Hemisphere and winter for the South, until 23rd September, the second equinox. The days begin to get shorter and the nights longer – Autumn for the Northern Hemisphere and Spring for the South.

From the 22nd December, the second solstice, the days begin getting longer. It is Winter for the Northern Hemisphere, Summer for the Southern. Nights continue to get shorter until 21st March – and the new equinox.

8 How is there a day and a night?

As the Earth travels around the sun, so it spins on its own axis.

The 24 hours it takes to spin on its axis is called a "day" – but, of course, this includes the night hours, too. And night-time varies with the seasons and also with the latitude.

At the Equator it always lasts twelve hours, and, as we get towards the Poles the duration varies until, at the Poles themselves, the nights are six months long!

9 What is a year?

A year is the time the Earth takes to travel around the sun and lasts 365 and a quarter days, according to the "solar calendar". But to make the calendar and everything else easier, we have an ordinary year lasting 365 days. The quarter days are then added up, and every four years we have an extra day, making a Leap Year of 366 days.

It was not always like this. Some people used the Moon as an "astroguide", setting their year at 12 lunar months. But 12 lunar months are shorter than a solar year – so the Moon or Lunar Year finished out of step with the seasonal rhythm of the Earth.

For example – we know that the 20th March is the beginning of Spring in the Northern Hemisphere; but if we had a Lunar Year, which is shorter than the Solar Year, our 21st March would no longer be the day of equinox.

So instead of seeing 21st March as the first day of Spring, we would find ourselves in the middle of winter!

10 What are time zones?

When the sun is at its highest, we say it is mid-day or noon.

But, the Earth is round – so mid-day does not arrive for everyone at the same time. In the east it arrives earlier than in the west.

If we divide the circumference of the Earth (around 41,000 kilometres) by twenty-four hours, we find that one hour equals 1,700, going from east to west. So, when it is twelve o'clock in Rome, it is eleven o'clock going east to Paris – and three o'clock going west to Ankara in Turkey.

But also in towns in the same country – Manchester and London, Bonn and Berlin, Barcelona and Seville – mid-day comes at slightly different times.

So, each country had to fix a time for all clocks to show throughout the nation.

These times were fixed at a convention in 1884 when it was decided to sub-divide the Earth into 24 zones.

The same time applies in all areas of these zones, calculated by the distance from longitude 0° at Greenwich.

11 What is a temperature range?

A temperature range is the difference in temperatures. It can be daily, between day and night; monthly, between the hottest and coldest days; or a yearly temperature range between the coldest and hottest months.

All differences in temperatures increase with the latitude and distance from the sea. The Sahara Desert, for example, has a daily temperature range, because it is so hot by day, yet very cold at night.

12 What is the hottest place on Earth?

Maximum temperatures are recorded at the Sahara Desert.

And the hottest cities? According to the hottest months on average, the hottest city in Europe is Athens, with 26.8° Celsius, followed by Madrid, with 24.7° Celsius, then Rome with 24.6° Celsius.

In Africa, it is Khartoum with 33.1° Celsius, then Cairo with 28.6° Celsius. In Central America, the hottest city is New Orleans with 27.4° Celsius, with Buenos Aires in South America – 23.1° Celsius.

In Asia, Baghdad registers an average 34.4° Celsius, then New Delhi, with 33.4° Celsius.

In the Pacific, the hottest city is Honolulu with 25.3° Celsius, followed by Sydney, Australia – 22° degrees and Melbourne with 19.8° Celsius.

The mildest winters are recorded in Africa. At Kinshasa, the temperature stays at over 22° Celsius, followed by Honolulu then Rio de Janiero, where temperatures never fall below 21° Celsius.

13 What is the coldest place on Earth?

The coldest place on Earth is the Antarctic, where temperatures can often go as low as 78° below zero, Celsius!

Then comes Siberia with 50.1° Celsius below zero.

The coldest cities in Europe, based on average temperatures during the coldest months, are Archangel in Russia with 13.3° Celsius below zero, followed by Montreal, Canada, with 10.6°, Beijing with 4.7° and Tashkent with 1.3°.

14 What are grottos?

Grottos are natural hollows either in the ground or mountain-sides. Many have special features.

Long, long ago, water rich in limestone fell to Earth and filtered through the surface of these grottos.

As this water evaporated, it left behind deposits of lime-stone.

The continuous dripping of water, and so the build-up of limestone formed stalagmites – cones or columns of calcite.

But some drops of water – and so, the limestone – stayed at the top, or "face" of the grotto, building up to form stalactites, which hung down, as well as the stalagmites, which rose up.

The result of this very slow but continuous action created some spectacular sights... columns, needles, curtains and walls..... No human being could design or reproduce such fairy-tale landscapes.

Some of the most spectacular grottos are in Portugal, Yugoslavia and Castellana in Italy, as well as Mammut in the United States.

15 What are speliologists?

Speliologists study grottos – natural hollows which are longer than wider – and caves, which are the opposite.

Speliologists go underground or inside mountains, measuring, taking photographs, collecting samples. They are interested in the origins of the grottos and caves, their size and formation, the minerals of which they are formed, the animals and plants which lived there, the fossilised remains of man and weather conditions.

Many animals sheltered and took refuge in caves – insects, crustaceans (crabs, lobsters, etc.) worms, spiders, molluscs (snails, mussels, etc.) bats, mice and amphibians.

Cave-dwelling animals developed an excellent sense of touch, also losing the natural colours of their skin and sometimes their sight, the further from the mouth of the cave they went.

And the nearer they lived to the entrance, the more they were like those who lived on the outside.

16 What is the Grand Canyon?

The Grand Canyon in Colorado, U.S.A. is a series of huge gorges "dug out" by the waters of the Colorado River rushing through a narrow tract joining Little Colorado to Lake Mead.

Over 2,000 metres deep, up to 25 kilometres wide and 450 kilometres long, the Colorado began this canyon five or six million years ago. And as well as tourists, it attracts the adventurous types who ride down it in rubber dinghies.

17 Which are the longest rivers in the world?

The longest rivers are found where there are vast areas through which they can flow.

In contrast to the rivers flowing through the huge expanses of great continents of Asia, Africa and America, those in Europe are shorter and narrower.

But these rivers flow through some of the most densely populated areas of the world, with castles and houses on banks which are linked by bridges and ferries, serving almost all types of trade.

The longest river is the Nile – 6,670 kilometres long, followed by the Mississippi-Missouri, 6,420 kilometres, and the Upper Amazon, 6,280 kilometres. Next is the Yangtse – 5,800 kilometres; the Ob-Irtysh, Russia, 5,410 kilometres; the Rio de la Plata, Argentina, 4,700; the Mekong, 4500 kilometres; and Russia's Volga, 3,530 kilometres.

For a long European river, we come down to 2,860 kilometres for the Danube, 1,020 for the Rhine, and 1,020 for the Loire.

18 Which are the highest mountains on Earth?

The highest mountain is Everest (8,848 metres). Dhaulagiri, Nanga Parbat, Kanchenjunga and Annapurna, also in the Himalayas between India and China, are around 8,000 metres. In Argentina the Aconcagua is 6960 metres, with others over 6,000 metres. Alaska's McKinley is 6,194 metres high; Kenya's Kilimanjaro is 5,199 metres. In Antarctica, Vinson is 5,140 metres. Highest in Europe is Mont Blanc (4,810).

19 Where are the highest waterfalls in the world?

Water from the Carino River in Venezuela falls from a height of a good 972 metres at Angel's Falls, the world's highest waterfall. Second highest is Tugela in South Africa at 948 metres, and third Yosemite, 739 metres. Then comes Utigard in Norway with 610 metres, and the Sutherland Falls in New Zealand, 579, formed by the waters of the river Roaring Creek.

There are also a number of European Falls – the French Garvarnie, 421 metres; Krimmler in Austria, (381 metres); and in Switzerland, Staubbach (305 metres) and Giessbach (300 metres), Norway's Mardalsfoss, 297 metres and Vetti, 260 metres. Then comes the only falls in Asia, the Gersoppa in India, with 253 metres.

Yet it is not the height which makes Falls famous. The African Victoria Falls, fed by the Zambesi river is only 122 metres.

And the much-celebrated Niagara Falls between Canada and the U.S.A. is only 51 metres!

20 How was coal made?

In the story of our Earth, there was once the Carboniferous Age. This began about 350 million years ago and lasted 80 million years! All this time, millions and millions of plants and trees grew, then died. And, as they rotted, they slowly turned into thick beds of peat.

As the levels of water rose on our planet, the layers of peat were covered with mud and sand from the sea, sealing the peat off from the air and gradually changing it into coal.

The forests of the Carboniferous Age were formed by ferns as big as trees and huge plants.

Here lived spiders, scorpions, giant dragon-flies, and in the swamps, fish, plants – and amphibians who could live on land as well as in water.

Other animals became water creatures, developing legs to swim.

When the Carboniferous Age came to an end, the swamps which for millions of years accumulated the coal we use today saw the arrival of dinosaurs.

21 How many types of mines are there?

By the word "mining", we mean a deposit of useful minerals and the equipment necessary to bring them up out of the Earth.

There are open cast mines, with men using excavators, bulldozers etc. and underground mines, where two or more vertical shafts have to be dug, with a network of tunnels branching off from each.

As well as coal mines, there are salt mines (for rock salt) mines for iron, sulphur, diamonds, talc, kaolin... and mines for liquids and gases, such as oil and methane, usually called "wells" and "fields".

The U.S.A. and Russia are the biggest producers of coal.

But the richest areas in Europe are Britain, Belgium, the German Ruhr and Poland – the Northern Central area of Europe.

The question and answer for 20 March explains how coal was formed.

So, if we could turn back the clock 300 million years, we would see dinosaurs and ferns as high as houses on the streets of of our mining towns!

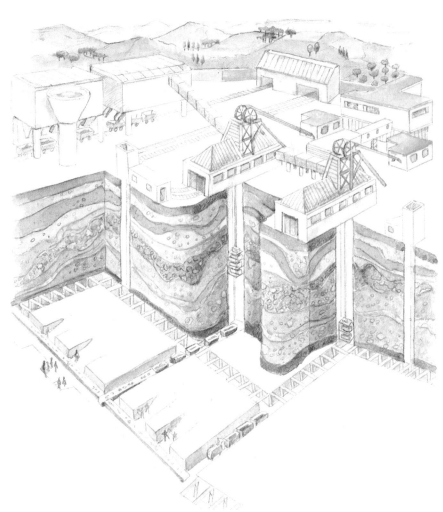

22 Where was the first oil well?

Until mid 19th century, oil could only be collected on the surface, mixed with water from wells.

But as science and invention forged ahead, so the demands from the expanding industry increased.

In 1850 a way was found of extracting, from coal and petroleum, kerosene – a liquid fuel which burnt slowly, giving an excellent source of light.

But as the demands for lighting increased, the small quantities of petroleum taken from water were not enough to produce the amounts of kerosene required. So the American Edwin Drake had the idea of digging a well to reach the petroleum and pump it up to the surface. On 27th August 1859 at Titusville, Pennsylvania, Drake dug the first oil well to begin the petroleum age.

And when the motor car arrived, working on benzine, derived from petroleum, this new industry became one of the most important in the world.

23 What is an oil rig?

All over the world, television reports brought us pictures of the oil rigs in Kuwait as they burned the marine installations which bring up gas and petroleum from the sea bed.

These fires are fed from underground deposits of petroleum and a natural gas called methane.

Like coal, petroleum also has quite a past.

It began forming at the beginning of the dinosaur age, building up in gigantic "tanks" or reservoirs.

A complete oil rig installation drills through three layers – of methane, petroleum and salt water – usually separated by intermediate rock. By drilling through the first layer, it will reach the natural gas of methane.

Then, going through the rocky base below the gas, the drilling will reach petroleum.

Finally, by going through the the rocky base of the layer of petrol, the drilling arrives at salt water – the remains of the prehistoric oceans in which plants and animals once lived.

24 What is a water table?

When rain falls, it soaks into the ground, through gaps in soil and rock. When it can go no further, it forms a water table.

And when water is within a layer of loose gravel or rock sandwiched between two layers of sloping, solid rock, the water is forced to flow down, squeezed by the rocky layers. So, when it meets an outlet, the water spurts up to the surface.

This is phenomenon is called an Artesian Well.

With a layer of rock underneath only, it is called the phreatic table, with water flowing naturally, as a spring.

If a spring is very deep, particularly in volcanic areas, the water spurting up is hot. This water table is called a Geothermal and the springs geysers.

So, different man-made wells are needed to draw water from the different tables.

A well for the phreatic table simply draws water but a man-made artesian well has to be drilled through rock and the flow of water controlled.

25 How is a glacier formed?

In places where there is a lot of snow, and the temperature does not rise much above freezing, even in summer, the snow cannot melt.

Instead, it accumulates and turns into ice – and when the ice accumulates it forms a glacier.

Like a great river, a glacier may eventually slide down a slope, forging a path to form a U-shaped valley.

Boulders, rocks and stones fall in and get carried along – and when the front of the glacier gets beyond the snow-covered areas and the ice begins to melt, all these rocks and stones are left in a rounded heap, called a "moraine".

The remainder of the glacier continues on its way, carrying great masses of unbroken ice. These will be ice-bergs when they reach the sea and finally begin to melt.

The force of these heavy rivers of ice is particularly visible in Scandinavia, where the fjords bear witness to the power of the ancient glaciers.

26 Where are the biggest glaciers?

Added together, all glaciers cover an area of around 15,000,000 square kilometres – equal to 10% of the Earth's surface!

Most are in Antarctic and Greenland – but it is Iceland, an island of around 103,000 square kilometres which has three of the biggest glaciers.

Vatnajokull, the world's largest, has an area of 8,800 square kilometres and is 150 kilometres long; Hofsjokull, sixth biggest at 1,350 square kilometres (36 kilometres long) and Langjokull, eighth biggest in the world, with an area of 1300 square kilometres and a length of 55 kilometres.

The second largest glacier is at Malaspina, Alaska, covering an area of 3,800 square kilometres, then Russia's Novaja Zemlja, with 3,000 square kilometres.

In Europe, the highest mountain range is the Alps, with a total of 500 square kilometres of glacier.

Of these, the Aletsch glacier is the biggest, 38 kilometres long.

27 What are National Parks?

Wherever in the world we find large areas of outstanding natural beauty, the State will decide that they are worthy of special attention and give money to pay for their protection and upkeep.

These areas are called National Parks, protected by special laws and run by specially-appointed administrators.

The plants, flowers, trees and animal life of the National Parks are inspected and surveyed by rangers.

There are generally regulations which apply to visitors – and building on the land is either restricted by a rigorous planning application procedure or simply not allowed at all.

The biggest National Parks are in America, Asia and Africa.

Largest is the huge Canadian National Park of Buffalo Wood, with over 45,000 square kilometres, followed by the slightly smaller Gobi in Mongolia, and the Etosha National Park in Namibia, covering an area of around 23,000 kilometres.

Next comes the Brazilian Neblina National Park, the Canadian Kluane and Baffin Island and the Kenyan Tsavo National Park – over 20,000 square kilometres.

Between 10,000 and 12,000 square kilometres, we find the Chilean O'Higgins Park, the island of Iona in the U.K., the Manu in Peru, and Jasper in Canada.

One of the most famous, Yellowstone Park, is "only" 9,400 square kilometres!

There are also marine National Parks to protect animal and plant life in the sea.

28 Where do we find the world's largest forests?

If they were put all together, the forests would take up more than a quarter of the Earth's surface!

Asia has the most, followed by South America, North America, Africa, Europe, then Australia.

The Asian jungles and the Amazon forests are largest, with thousands of different types of animals and plants – but so dense and thick, that even with all the methods man has at his disposal, they cannot be conquered.

29 How long did it take for the Earth to form?

Millions and millions of years ago, there was one vast continent in the Southern Hemisphere which scientists call "Gondwana".

Africa, South America, Australia and India – all gradually broke away from it and began moving northward. The mountains of the Himalayas formed where India joined on to Asia.

And the only part of the Gondwana which still remains is – the Antarctic.

30 When was it proved that the Earth was round?

On the 20th September 1519, five ships and 237 men left San Lucar in Spain, commanded by the Portuguese explorer, Ferdinand Magellan. They were bound for the spices of India – but instead of going west, as Columbus had in 1492, Magellan went south, along the little-explored African coast, before crossing the Atlantic.

One ship sank, another turned back – but Magellan carried on until he reached the southern-most tip of South America, sailing through the Straits named after him and into the Pacific Ocean.

The sacrifices and hardships were tremendous. But Magellan landed in the Philippines.

Here, attacked by natives, Magellan and many of his crew lost their lives.

But the journey continued. And in 1522, eighteen men returned home, including the Italian Antonio Pigafetta who wrote his "Report of the First Voyage Around The World" – the journey which had proved that the world was indeed round.

31 When did man first see the Earth?

On 16th July 1969, the American space-ship Apollo II was launched towards the Moon.

And on the 21st day of the Space Mission, American astronaut, Neil Armstrong set foot on the Moon's surface at the Bay of Tranquillity.

In front of their television sets, "Earth-men" could share in the emotions and the excitement, seeing before their eyes the Earth seeming to float against the black background of cosmic space.

AT HOME

In a Castle

In a Castle

LONG before sunrise, there's plenty going on in the castle!

By the light of candles and flaming torches, kitchen maids are melting cinders in boiling water, so that they can do the washing – the linen must be really clean, because the king is coming on a visit!

Each copper pot and pan must be polished with vinegar and sand from the river.

Stable-boys brush away the smallest spider's web from every corner of the stables. They check all the harness, setting aside anything which looks just a little too worn or may need mending. All the horses are being groomed.

And whilst Her Ladyship makes quite sure that they have everything needed for such a splendid occasion, the Castle Lord is checking the bridge over which the royal procession will pass. The commander of the guards tells his men exactly how they must follow his orders.

Everywhere, from the smallest courtyard to the keep of the castle, all is hustle and bustle. The basket-maker, carpenter, potter, blacksmith, weaver – everyone works hard.

There is a poet, too. He happened to be at the castle when news came of the king's visit, so he was invited to stay.

At the moment, he is talking to a monk from a nearby monastery who comes to teach His Lordship's children. He also gives lessons to young Charles.

And as the sky gets light and the sun rises, Charles cannot help being nervous. It is a special day for him, too. There is so much he wants to do – yet he hardly knows where to begin.

"Going somewhere, Charles?" enquires the monk.

"N-no..." Charles falters. "No, not really..."

The monk smiled as he turned to the poet.

"We shall be asking the king to make a knight of this young man!" announced the monk. "He has been an apprentice here since he was ten years old, now he is sixteen! His parents cannot come, because their castle is 300 leagues away and it would take so long to get here!"

"A future knight?" smiled the poet. "I must write a song in honour of the occasion!"

"A – a song?" Charles

stammered again. "For me? But I – I've done nothing to deserve it!"

"Well, you are only young!" chuckled the poet. "So you haven't lived long enough to have done much!"

"But I have been watching you," he continued more seriously. "I have seen what a good hunter you are, a fine horseman, too. I also saw what you did for a poor washer-woman. When a charcoal-burner dirtied her washing, you made him give her some charcoal to make up for what he did! You say

you have done nothing. But I say you have already done a great deal!"

"I agree!" said the monk, laying a hand on the boy's shoulder.

"You think so?" said Charles. He still seemed anxious. "I keep thinking I'm not ready to be a knight. I'm not tall enough, clever enough. Sometimes…" he hesitated, "sometimes I'm afraid, when I hear a wild boar in the forest, for instance. I wonder if I shall be able to use my sword.

My master has had to come to my aid two or three times…"

"Enough, enough!" the monk

broke in with a laugh. "These doubts only tell us that you think about what you do!"

"Now," he continued, "think about this. The master, myself and this gentleman, not to mention the stable-boys, the guards – and the master's youngest daughter – we all think you should now become a knight. If you say that we are wrong, then you also say that we are less wise than you! Is that so?"

"No!" Charles exclaimed. "I would never ever think that!"

"Then put your doubts to flight!" said the monk. "You have faith in us, now have faith in yourself! Spend some time before the king arrives thinking about what it really means to become a knight!"

The monk's voice had become very serious as he spoke. But with each word, every doubt Charles had seemed to disappear.

Now on his face was an expression of joy and pride, his eyes shining.

"Yes!" he cried, "To become a knight is a great honour! And I shall spend my life being worthy of it!"

1 When did men live in caves?

Caves were "houses" for people in prehistoric times. Inside, men made shelters, stretching animal skins over a frame-work of branches or building wooden huts.

If caves were found in a good position, or if one was near to another, men could live there for a long time.

At Balzi Rossi in Lugaria, Italy, traces of prehistoric men have been found dating from 150,000 to 10,000 years ago!

2 Were there any special caves?

Unlike animals, men have always had feelings, together with respect for life and the mysteries of birth and death.

Prehistoric man lived in a world which was often cruel – so they soon felt the need for ways to express their feelings of fear, hope and joy.

Certain caves were kept as "temples" for this purpose, where men would meet to find peace and companionship, learning to trust and depend on each other.

It was about 35,000 years ago that men began decorating these caves with huge paintings and carvings, which they believed would bring them good fortune and protect them – for example, before a hunt.

Some of the most beautiful of these caves have been found in the Pyrenees, between France and Spain.

One cave at a place called Lascaux was discovered by students in 1940. Here, the magnificent pictures were painted between 17,000 and 13,000 years B.C.

3 How were pile-dwellings built?

Pile-dwellings looked very much like Canadian log cabins of today, with roofs sloping down at either side and very low walls. They were built on a platform of wood, supported on long poles planted in the ground, often on the banks or even in the waters of a lake or a river.

The high raised platform was also a defence – not only against enemies, but also animals, especially rats and mice.

4 What is a village?

A village is a settlement for a small number of families – usually with just a school, a doctor, a church and a few shops. The village was the first form of community. And in countries such as Indonesia, South America and Africa, it is still the most common.

As well as villages in country areas, there are also those built specially by employers, holiday villages and "Olympic villages" to house competitors in the Games.

5 What is a city?

A city is a big community, with all the services needed not only by people living in the city itself, but also those who live around it.

There are bus and railway stations, links with motorways, schools, colleges and universities, hospitals and banks, police, fire and ambulance stations; factories, industrial estates, shopping centres with shops of all kinds which people visit from miles around.

Sometimes a city will have an airport, or even docks if the city is near to the sea. There are museums, art galleries, exhibition centres, public libraries and newspaper offices.

When there are more than a million people living in a city, it is called a "metropolis", which means "Mother City".

Everything centres around the city and more so the metropolis as far as the surrounding areas are concerned. Towns, villages, country areas… they all depend on the city for the services which are found there, with many people journeying into the city to work, school or hospital. So,

there have to be road and rail links to all parts, not just the centre.

The town often expands by extending buildings, streets and services to surrounding areas. But if this growth is uncontrolled, huge over-spill populations are created without any proper services, illegal or makeshift housing and a hard life for the people.

Examples of uncontrolled expansion are seen in such places as Mexico City, where the population is around 19,000,000 people and Cairo, whose population is 14,000,000.

6 What is the oldest city in the world?

Built in the Middle East and even recorded in The Bible as a fine city with a strong wall – Jericho was first built around 7,800 B.C. although it has been destroyed and built many times.

Its famous wall was a metre and a half thick at the top. The Bible tells how, after God had told him to get the people to change their wicked ways, Joshua sounded his horn – and the powerful wall crumbled and the city was conquered.

7 Why did the Red Indians live in tents?

When the first Europeans arrived in America, they found people who painted their bodies red – which is why explorer John Cabot first called them "Redskins" in 1497.

Many of these "Redskins" lived in tents made of animal skins and the reason for this was simple. The "Red Indians" – or North American Indian – might never be a farmer.

But, above all else, he was a skilled hunter, taking only what was necessary for food and using the skins for clothing and tents.

And these hunters could follow game, especially during the migration season.

Tents could be taken down and put up again very quickly, and so, following the bison to its winter pastures was not a problem for them – especially after the Europeans had also introduced the horse to America, an animal ideally suited to speed and hunting.

Before this, the North American Indians had travelled on foot, using dogs to carry their loads.

8 Did North American Indians build cities?

Not all North American Indians were wandering hunters. In Arizona and New Mexico there were communities who preferred farming. But they soon found tents were not really suitable for this life – which is why, in New Mexico, they built houses to form their own little cities, called "pueblos" (Spanish for "villages"). Built in a semi-circle with sun-dried bricks, the houses were like big buildings split into apartments.

9 Why did the Mongolian people live in tents?

Wanderers from ancient times, the people of Mongolia still live in tents today.

They have also bred animals for thousands of years, always moving on to find the best pastures for their herds of wild horses and camels. And because they live in a harsh climate, they make their tents of thick, heavy felt. These tents are called *yurts,* and are made in a cylinder shape with a cone at the top and a hole to act as a chimney.

These beautiful tents are furnished with rugs, and there is a proper door, always richly decorated.

Nowadays, Mongolians are gradually coming to live in cities and houses, but many prefer the unlimited space of the steppes of Asia, with more than half still nomads – wanderers.

Some Mongolians live in the part of China known as Inner Mongolia, and some in Eastern Mongolia, which is in Central Asia. This is a mountainous region, with vast, high plains, and the Gobi Desert.

With unlimited pasture-land in the enormous, wind-swept plains, farming is a tradition here, in the harsh climate which has discouraged any invasion from the east for centuries.

Only with the coming of railways have Mongolian people been able to reach "civilisation". They are descended from Genghis Khan, who led his horse-men to conquer half Asia, and of Kubla Khan, the emperor who welcomed the Venetian explorer, Marco Polo, to his magnificent court.

10 Was there central heating in the past?

Yes. Roman architects built houses and villas so that hot air coming from an outside furnace circulated through holes and gaps, under the floors and around the walls. Many people today think this system was kind to the environment because it did not pollute the atmosphere.

On the other hand, there are many who say it was less kind to the environment, because the hot air came from burning lots of wood.

11 When was glass first used for windows?

Glass is an ancient invention. But for a long time, so few people knew how to make it that only the very rich could afford a single piece. In the case of window panes, it was only when the art of glazing spread that the prices began to fall. But until the nineteenth century when glass began being made in factories and more people could afford it, most windows were closed with wooden shutters or panels of parchment.

12 What are houses in cold climates like?

In cold climates, there is more rain and snow than there is sun. So the houses have steep, sloping roofs, so that the snow can slide down from the top – otherwise there is a risk of the roof breaking under the weight!

The windows are small, to keep the warm air inside, and the cold air out. The walls are large and painted, to absorb as much heat as possible. Rooms are small and the beds are often four-poster.

In Russia, the beds are often mounted on big, ceramic heaters!

When it is cold, there are also fewer of the daylight hours which bring valuable heat from the sun. This is why, until quite recently, the kitchen was the main room of the house, getting heat and light at the same time.

Today, houses in many cold countries have central heating and electricity to give light all through the day. But not long ago, to read a book in the warm whilst it snowed and rained outside seemed like a miracle – not only at home, but also at school.

13 Is it cold or hot inside an igloo?

It is very cosy inside an igloo!

This is proved by the fact that eskimos build them in winter to keep out the cold! Inside, they are lined with animal skins, and a fire – for which they make a vent in the middle of the roof – keeps the igloo warm, as well as giving light and the means to cook food – although this last point is not so important. The name "eskimo" was given by neighbouring countries, and means "eaters of raw meat"!

14 How is an igloo built?

First, the eskimo cuts blocks of hard snow with a knife, building upwards in a spiral to make a dome shape. To keep a comfortable temperature, the eskimo then builds a passage-way, leading into a sort of outer room. Cold air then circulates in the passage-way and the outside room, warming up before reaching the living quarters. Food is kept in the outer room, where there is no fear of it going bad.

15 What about houses in hot countries?

Keeping warm in a cold country is a problem, and it is the same trying to keep cool indoors when it is hot outside.

Houses in hot countries have windows which are big and airy.

Roofs are fairly flat, where it is also possible to sleep at nights when it is really hot.

As with houses in cold countries, the walls are spacious – but painted white, to reflect the heat.

And when the house is built around a courtyard, there is often a water fountain in the middle. This not there as a decoration, but to refresh the air.

So the air which circulates around the fountain cools the water, the water cools the air – and so it goes on, with more air being continually cooled all around the fountain and so cooling the walls of the house.

In some hot countries houses are built with a verandah around the outside; this prevents the sun from shining directly onto the walls and encourages air to circulate around the building.

Inside houses in hot climates, the room in which there is the least activity is the kitchen – exactly the opposite to cold countries.

It is no fun being anywhere near ovens, which is why women often cook outside, in the open.

This is quite an ancient custom. Archaeologists have found in tombs of Ancient Egyptians round loaves of bread with grains of sand inside – evidence that the women of Ancient Egypt preferred cooking out in the open.

16 Why were castles built in the Middle Ages?

We only have to look at castles to see why they were such a good defence for noblemen and their estates against enemies.

Castles were always built on a high, dominating position, with the first signs of danger seen easily. When this happened, the people on the estates would gather within the strong walls of the castle and pull up the drawbridge, preventing the enemy from crossing the deep waters of the castle moat.

17 What brought about the end of castles?

Each part of the castle served as a special defence. There was its position and high, strong walls.

Then there was the wide moat filled with water which could only be crossed when the drawbridge was down.

Little light came in through the slits in the walls, made so that arrows could be fired.

The towers at each corner controlled all sides of the building. The terraces had battlements to protect the people inside.

All this was very effective against the spears and arrows of attackers at ground level.

Then in 1346 came the Battle of Crecy – the first of the Hundred Years War between France and England.

Here, cannon fire was used in open country for the first time. After this, it was soon seen that the castle's defences and the strongest castle wall offered little protection when such powerful weapons were being fired at them from a distance.

18 Why were monasteries built in the Middle Ages?

In the 6th century, Europe was plagued by hordes of cruel people and life was very hard.

But at this time, monks prayed and worked peacefully in woods and fields – and so the monasteries offered a refuge for people, with prayers to comfort the soul and home-grown food to eat.

Monasteries spread throughout Europe, becoming as much a part of the landscape of the Middle Ages as the castles were.

19 What lighting was used before electricity?

We are now so used to the electric light, it is hard to believe that this victory over darkness happened only a century ago. Before this, for thousands of years, people used the flame as a light.

Cavemen lit torches of slow-burning wood. Later on, there were little oil lamps in which a wick dipped in oil or grease burned slowly, with lamps and lanterns of various types coming next.

Then, in the first centuries of Christianity, there were beautiful white candles made of beeswax.

After that, things remained largely unchanged for hundreds of years, but with people using every scrap of light – for example, using a mirror above a fireplace to reflect the light.

In the 19th century, paraffin lamps came on the scene.

But when the light bulb was invented, the thousand-year battle against darkness was over.

Now, people could switch a light on and off!

20 Where was Venice built?

A lagoon is a stretch of salt water coming in from the sea.

It often forms around an island, and is separated from the open sea by a low sand-bank.

At the end of the sixth century the Venetian lagoon was not very nice, and only a few people lived on the island.

The salt water made it difficult for anything to grow, the tides and flooding were a constant threat, which in turn meant that the link with the mainland was uncertain and often very dangerous.

But Venice did have some advantages.

Fish and salt could be obtained from the sea, and the difficult connection with the mainland was also a good defence – a fact discovered by people fleeing from invasion to Grado, another Italian town built on a lagoon island.

In fact, Venice was largely populated by people from Grado, as more and more refugees fled from the mainland to settle there.

Unfortunately, many of the buildings in Venice are now in danger of sinking into the sea.

27

21 Which ancient city was like Venice?

On the 8th November 1519, Spanish invaders led by Hernan Cortes landed in Tenochtitlan, capital of the ancient Aztecs. The city had been built on an island in the centre of a lake, connected to the mainland by a raised-up pathway.

Temples, palaces and gardens could be seen in the distance, boats crowding the lake. It was a city on water, like Venice – but not so lucky. It was destroyed and Mexico City founded in its place.

22 Were there people who lived in trees?

Well – in the story-books, Tarzan lived in a tree, and so did Peter Pan!

And there are still some trees which are thought to be the "door" to an underground shelter or tunnel, used as an escape from danger. King Charles I is said to have hidden from the Roundheads in a tree, there are many stories of trees in Sherwood Forest giving shelter to Robin Hood and his men before they set off to battle against the soldiers of King John.

But, however nice we may imagine it to be, it is not easy to fulfil the dream of building a house and living amid the greenery, along with the birds.

Yet one English woman did see that dream come true. She got the idea of building a tree house, the only one of its kind in the world, when she lived in Kenya, Africa, with her husband. She called it "Treetops", and it gave her the opportunity of watching the wild animals at night, as they came to drink and wandered around below.

23 Are there floating cities?

Where the possibilities of finding homes on the mainland are slim – or non-existent – "boat people" can often form a "floating city", every bit as industrious as those on land.

Most famous, perhaps, is in Hong Kong, where the floating city is concentrated around the port of Sai Kung, where thousands of people have lived for generations in their traditional and highly colourful sampan crafts.

24 Which is the most famous palace in the world?

The French King Louis XIV decided to build a palace at Versailles, about 20 kilometres from Paris, where his father had built a castle.

Very grand and beautiful, the castle became a magnificent palace, surrounded by forests – a sort of royal village with statues and buildings, parks and avenues, fountains and works of art. In 1682, Louis brought his court and his government to Versailles and for a hundred years, France was governed from there.

25 How many people lived at Versailles?

The Versailles estate covered more than one hundred hectares (almost 250 acres), and was originally planned to house a royal court and a government.

At the height of its glory, ten thousand people lived there, with 2,500 horses in the magnificent stables.

In the palace itself there was a splendid theatre, a chapel and many apartments, as well as the great Royal Apartment, with its six magnificent sitting rooms and where the king received the court three times a week.

Receptions were held in the famous Gallery of Mirrors, 75 metres long and 10 metres wide, with more than three thousand lights reflected in the mirrors which covered the walls.

King Louis also had all the furniture for the Gallery of Mirrors made of solid silver.

The palace at Versailles was so vast that there was room in the middle of the park for another, smaller palace, where the king could rest from all the hard work and stress at court.

26 When was the lift invented?

In the 19th century, houses began to be built higher and higher, because of the numbers of people coming to work in the cities, and the shortage of land for building. So, lifts had to be introduced, working first by a hand-driven winch, and then, in 1880 by an electric motor. The first safety device was invented by the American engineer Otis, whereby the "cage" did not move if a cable broke, so preventing it from falling.

27 How does a lightning conductor work?

A lightning conductor is a metal pole which is set into the ground, going up the side of a building to the roof. In a storm, the air is full of electricity – charges of this electricity are what we call lightning. It is attracted to the points of objects – so the tip of the conductor attracts the lightning, taking it down to earth, and the building is not struck. The lightning conductor was invented by the American Benjamin Franklin in 1752.

28 When was the flush toilet invented?

Until about 150 years ago, all waste went straight into the earth and toilets were just holes in the ground.

Up high, waste was thrown out to run down the hillside, away from the house.

But, for anyone below, there was always the danger of a makeshift "toilet" being emptied overhead!

In the towns, streets smelled foul. And in some larger cities such as Paris, there were little gutters at the sides of the roads.

Today, gutters drain only water, but once they drained everything!

Towards the end of the 18th century, people began to be more aware of the smell, the poor hygiene everywhere and how all this led to poor health.

And after a few attempts at the beginning of the 19th century, the first toilets were installed in England – an improvement introduced in old houses, and built by law in new houses, with sewers and water systems quickly extending to all parts of the country.

29 When did electricity come into our homes?

12th January 1882 saw the first public electricity supply in London. At first, the supply was limited.

But during the following years, the service was improved and before too long many miles of wire were connecting homes to the electricity power stations.

And wherever the electricity network cannot reach, a supply can be obtained with batteries or generators, so that electricity can come into all our homes today.

THE SEA

Adventure at the Lighthouse

Adventure at the Lighthouse

TOM LOOKED glumly out of the window, watching the angry sea hurling itself against the shores of the island.

The wind was stronger than he had ever known it, shaking some trees as if they would break, uprooting others and throwing them where it pleased. The sky was grey and it was bitterly cold.

"Tomorrow morning," said Tom's grandpa, "I shall go and put a lamp on the shore. Perhaps we can get the electricity generator working… "The radio sat silently in a corner. No water came from the taps either.

"Can I come, too?" cried Tom.

His grandpa and mother looked at him. They knew he was getting bored after being cooped up in the house for the three days that the storm had already lasted. Flick the dog was bored, as well.

"All right," said Grandpa at last. "You can come!"

It was only just daybreak as the two prepared to leave, well wrapped up from head to foot, with Grandpa carrying his lantern and acetylene gas in a bag.

Whistling to the dog, he opened the door.

On the island there was a lighthouse which at one time was on a nautical chart, before it was put out of service.

But Tom's grandpa, a lighthouse keeper all his life, did not want "outside work", and by night he would often light up the bank with his lantern, just in case this might save some fisherman from smashing his boat against the rocks

Tom followed his grandpa. It was hard work walking against the wind, but he was happy to get out of the house for a while.

Suddenly, above the unending cry of the wind and the sea, they heard Flick barking. Hurrying towards the sound of his howls, they found him near a bush.

"Somebody's there!" cried Grandpa. He bent down, brushing aside his wet hair to see the pale face of a fisher boy, his lips blue.

"Run back home with Flick as fast as you can!" he shouted to Tom. "Bank up the fire, fetch blankets, milk and hot water and put a mattress near the fire!

Hurry!"

Tom set off as fast as he could, very nearly throwing himself indoors, he was so breathless.

Between pants, he told his mother what had happened. And by the time Grandpa burst in through the door, his mother was ready with a warm blanket to cover the boy. Then she carried him towards the fire, wiping him dry with warm towels until his skin began to get pinker.

Very slowly, the colour crept back to the boy's cheeks, and he began breathing deeply, talking feverishly.

"We must get the fever down," said Mother. "Otherwise he's going to be very ill indeed!"

She dissolved some pills into a mug of hot milk which she made the boy drink. Then she laid him down to sleep.

Tom slept too, quite worn out.

When he woke up, he saw his mother and grandpa helping the boy to drink some more milk with pills in it. Now there was more colour in his face, with two spots of pink on his cheeks.

"Is he better?" he asked.

"Not yet," said Grandpa. "Tonight will be the turning point."

Every hour, Mother checked the boy's temperature and gave him the warm milk. Supper was eaten in silence, except for the sounds of the wind, the sea and the storm. Then the fisher-boy began tossing and turning, sweating, mumbling, then shouting so much, they had a struggle to keep him covered. It was midnight before he began to get calmer.

"The boy is still fighting," Mother told Tom. "But he is young and strong. I think he'll pull through!" And as she prepared to spend the night by the boy's side, Tom slipped into an uneasy sleep, in the armchair. He was woken by a cry from his mother.

"Is – is he going to die?" he whispered, his eyes on the boy's pale face.

"No," she smiled, "the fever has gone. He's sleeping peacefully!"

Just then, a crackling noise made them jump. The radio was working again! None of them had noticed that the storm was over!

33

1 Why is the sea salty?

All water contains salt. The taste depends on the quantity and the water in which it is dissolved. In the sea, the saltiness depends on the temperature, the rivers flowing into it and the currents. With high temperatures, water evaporates and the salt gets very concentrated. Rivers bring clear water – so a sea which has a lot of river water has less salt than one where few rivers flow. The currents mix the waters and so dilutes the quantity of salt.

2 Which sea has the most salt?

The saltiest sea is the Dead Sea. In fact, it is an enormous lake, in a very hot region of the Middle East.

So, its waters evaporate a lot – and, as no rivers flow into it, the Dead Sea is very salty indeed!

In each litre of water there is a good 240 grammes of salt – enough to stop almost everything growing anywhere else, which is why it is called the "Dead" Sea.

The one advantage is that you can float on top, like a cork!

The quantity of salt in open seas varies – from about 8 grammes per litre of water from the Baltic Sea, to 37 grammes in the Atlantic Ocean, 39 in the Mediterranean and around 41 grammes in the Red Sea, the saltiest of all actual seas in the world.

The salts mostly present in sea waters are chlorine and sodium – sodium chloride, a compound of chlorine and sodium is the salt we use at home – zinc, magnesium, calcium and potassium, as well as smaller quantities of other salts.

3 How deep is the sea?

The Pacific Ocean is the deepest, with a minimum depth of 4,050 metres, maximum 11,030. Next is the Indian Ocean – minimum 3,900 metres, maximum 9,200 – and the Atlantic – minimum 3,300, maximum 9,200. The maximum depth of the Arctic Ocean is 5,500 metres, then the Mediterranean Sea with a maximum depth of 5,120 metres, minimum 1,000. Bottom of the deep sea league is the Baltic – minimum depth 460 metres and the North Sea – 90-100 metres.

4 What colour is the sea?

Sea waters are clear, but the surface colour depends on the reflection of the sky. So with a grey sky, the sea will be grey. And most of us have seen the leaden colour of the sea in bad weather.

But the deeper the water, the deeper the colour, becoming blue then gradually darkening into violet.

This is because the light from the rays of the sun are made up of all the gradual changes or "graduations" in colour.

These graduations are "lost", one by one, as the light cuts through the water.

The first colours to go, at depths of around 150 – 120 metres – the limit for all marine life which feeds on green plants – is yellow and red. At around 500 metres depth, we lose the blue and violet rays, then at a depth of 800 metres, the deep purple.

After that, all is darkness. This is where the meat-eating fish and animals live, those who feed on the remains which fall from the higher water levels.

5 How much of our planet is covered by water?

Added together, all the oceans and seas cover around two thirds of the Earth's surface.

The total surface of our planet is calculated at 510,000,000 square kilometres, of which the sea takes up about 372,000,000 square kilometres.

But this area would increase still more if we were to count the frozen glacier regions.

The quantity of water on the Earth does not always stay the same.

By the time The Ice Age ended over two million years ago the quantity of water on our planet was reduced so much that the level of the seas went down by about 140 metres.

This explains how it is that fossils of fish have been found well inland and on mountains, because these were the ancient inhabitants of the prehistoric seas. So there is not so much water on the Earth today as there used to be.

But if all the glaciers on Earth were to melt, the level of the seas would go up by at least 70 metres!

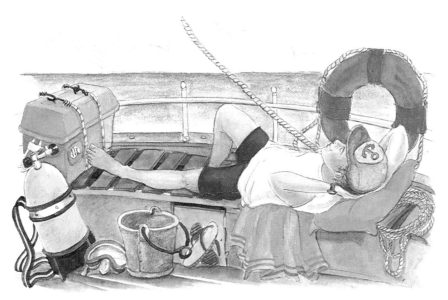

6 How can we avoid sea sickness?

Sickness, giddiness, sweating and headache are all symptoms of Sea Sickness. It is caused by the rolling of the boat around the longitudinal axis – from one broad-side to the other, or port to starboard, and around the horizontal axis – from bow to stern.

To avoid sea sickness, eat only solid, spicy food, and keep to the centre of the boat, in the open air, eyes closed to avoid looking at anything which is moving.

7 What sort of treasure can you find in the sea?

All things found in the sea have drifted along the sea bed or the coast.

When anyone finds a wreck, they must tell the authorities and give up any objects which are found. Whoever discovers the wreck has the right to be paid, as well as a reward, which varies according to whether it is found along the coast or in the open sea. Archaeological treasures are often found in European waters – especially the Mediterranean.

One of the most famous finds consisted of two magnificent bronze statues discovered by Italian frogmen. These were of warriors, each weighing 400 kilogrammes and made in 5 B.C. Bronze statues are not found every day, but amphoras (Roman wine-jars made of stone), vases, plates and coins often are. Whoever finds such treasures cannot keep them because they belong to everyone, and so it is right that they should be kept on display in museums, where everyone can see them.

8 Are there any sea monsters?

Hundreds of sea monsters have been reported, of every size and description. But not a single one has ever been captured.

We have to remember that when sailors spend months at sea, with time to look out on the expanse of the oceans, imagination can play strange tricks.

And when science or technology cannot give an explanation, out-of-the-ordinary sightings often lead to legends of sea monsters.

9 How many oceans are there?

The oceans are huge masses of water between continents – but all linked together to form one mass. There are three. The most easterly is the Pacific Ocean, covering about 100,000,000 square kilometres; then comes the Atlantic, with around 106,000,000 square kilometres and the Indian Ocean – around 75,000,000, plus the two glacier seas of the Arctic and the Antarctic, covering 70% of the Earth's surface, altogether.

10 Where do we find fjords?

Fjords are a special part of some coastlines. They are found in mountainous areas which were most deeply frozen over during the Ice Age, when huge glaciers spread from the North and South Poles, covering the Earth.

In some places, the ice bored deeply into the mountains, making steep valleys which went into the Earth for many kilometres.

Then, when the Ice Age ended, the ice melted, filling the valleys with water.

Fjords are a feature of the coasts of Scandinavia and Central America. They are also found in Alaska, Iceland and parts of Scotland.

The name "fjord" comes from a Scandinavian word meaning "door". This is because fjords, being so wide and deep, are easy for ships to sail through, as well as offering shelter from bad weather, danger or enemies.

Many times, the fjords hid the slender shapes of ships belonging to the fearless Viking warriors.

11 How do deep sea fish live?

Deep sea fish live completely in the dark, where green plants cannot grow. They have to withstand a strong water pressure and intense cold. For this reason, many have luminous parts to their bodies. Others have eyes trained to pick up the tiniest glow or speck of light. Others are blind, relying on their powers of touch and many have very thick skins. All feed on remains floating down from the surface and on other marine life.

12 What are tides?

Tides are movements of the Earth's waters, caused by attraction to the moon.

When part of the Earth is closest to the moon, the water becomes attracted to it, and so rises up twice a day – every 12 hours or so. This is high tide, with low tide following six hours after.

All waters are affected by tides, but high and low tides inland are minimal. Along the coasts of Britain, Alaska and South America, levels of up to 15 metres have been recorded, reaching a height of 22 metres along the Canadian coast. Whereas the water level at high tide in Venice seldom reaches more than half a metre.

Tides also vary according to the phases of the moon. In the first and last quarters, the difference between high and low tides is at its lowest, and highest when the moon is new or full. There is also a phase between a swelling tide and a falling tide, when the sea level remains constant.

13 What is a sea-quake?

Just as there are earthquakes, so there are sea-quakes, with vibrations in the water like an earthquake or the eruption of a volcano at the bottom of the sea.

On the high seas, this movement can be fairly light, sometimes just hitting against a ship or shaking it a little.

And although they can sometimes cause damage, this is rarely serious.

The movement of the water can produce waves which "travel" and crash some distance away.

When they meet obstacles, such as a shallow sea bed or the Earth's surface, these waves become huge, crashing down on anything in their path at a speed of 100 metes per second, with the force of a twenty or thirty-ton block of cement.

The worst sea-quakes have been those which occurred with earthquakes – in Lisbon, Portugal in 1755 and Messina, Sicily, in 1908, with waves 15 metres high, and the 1896 sea-quake of Kamaishi, Japan, with waves more than 30 metres high!

14 What causes a hurricane?

Hurricanes, cyclones, typhoons... all three words mean more or less the same – a formation on the oceans of zones of low pressure which cause changes of position in the air, generating violent winds which often approach speeds of over 120 kilometres an hour.

Fortunately for us, light tremors of the ground warn us of hurricanes approaching, and this usually helps us to forsee their arrival a few days beforehand.

15 What does a person need to go underwater?

The second rule of Archimedes says that a body immersed in liquid gets a push from the bottom towards the top equal to the weight of the water displaced...

In simple words – things float!

So, whoever goes underwater must have the equipment to prevent themselves rising upwards. They have to realise, too, that the deeper they go, the colder it gets, with the pressure of water increasing.

They also need air to breathe, to be able to move quickly, and defend themselves when necessary.

The underwater diver needs a rubber wet suit to keep out the cold and flippers for ease of movement.

Then comes the mask with a mouth-piece connected to an oxygen cylinder, or "air bottle", a life-jacket and ballast belt with weights to help keep the diver underwater.

Then there are the instruments – a manometer with which the diver controls the amount of air coming in from the oxygen cylinder, a depth-meter to tell the diver how far below the surface of the water he is, and an underwater watch to check the time spent down there.

All these measurements can now be put into an underwater computer which does all the calculations and gives out the information needed – far better than aqua-divers having to carry little slates and special pencils as they once did!

But hunting with the aid of oxygen cylinders is forbidden, as it is not fair to the fish.

16 Why do oysters make pearls?

Pearls are a form of defence used by oysters. When something strange gets into its shell, the oyster covers the intruder with layers of a material which it produces. So the pearl is nothing more than a beautiful container!

Pearls are so beautiful that men soon thought of ways to copy this natural way of producing them. Japanese breeders insert foreign bodies into the oyster shell to make the oyster form a pearl around it.

17 Where was the first light-house?

The first light-house was built on a little island called Pharos, off the coast of Egypt. And after Alexander the Great joined it up to the city, the Pharoahs of Egypt built a proper tower.

The light-house of Alexandria, completed in 280 B.C. was one of the ancient seven wonders of the world. It was 120 metres high with enormous braziers inside burning oil or wood. These lights were visible 50 kilometres away, a distance which increased when huge, metal mirrors were erected around the braziers to reflect the flames.

The Romans built many more light-houses, and one built at the time of the Emperor Caligula in 41 B.C. at the Channel port of Boulogne in France stayed in service until the end of the 17th century!

The Romans also erected two light-houses at Dover, the remains of which can still be seen today. But perhaps the most famous of all modern light-houses is the Statue of Liberty in New York Harbour.

18 Are salmon good swimmers?

An average salmon is about one and a half metres long and weighs 50 kgs.

They live in the ocean. But to reproduce, they return to the calm waters in which they were born. These "nurseries" can be up to 1,000 kilometres away – but that does not matter to the salmon as they set off on their long swim. The moment they reach the calm waters, they stop feeding, relying on their reserves of fat and their powerful muscles to leap through the water.

19 Are jellyfish dangerous?

Jellyfish are sea creatures, usually with mushroom-shaped bodies and tentacles which can sometimes sting and cause injury.

In Australia, there is one type of jellyfish which can cause the death of a man within minutes!

The Common Jellyfish is relatively harmless, despite its transparent body being up to half a metre wide! But swimmers can get painful stings from the "Portuguese Man of War" jellyfish which looks like an upturned boat.

20 Can we eat algae?

Algae – or seaweed – is all around us, and we do eat it!

There is an amazing variety of seaweed in all shapes, colours and sizes, and they live everywhere – on snow and volcanic soil, in puddles, walls and the cracks of a flower vase. All they need is a little warmth! In the sea, they form the beginning of a food chain – eaten by crustaceans such as lobsters and crabs, which are eaten by fish, which in turn are eaten by whales, birds, seals, bears – or humans.

Seaweed also gives oxygen to the water, helping other forms of life. And man soon learned to use it as a fertiliser for the earth, fodder for animals and food for himself.

In Asia, seaweed is farmed for food, and in Scandinavia, red seaweed jam is a real delicacy.

From seaweed we also get substances which are used in pharmaceutical industries, textiles and rubber, and to make explosives, toothpaste... even ice cream!

21 What is sargasso?

Sargasso is a brown algae or seaweed, mostly concentrated in mid-Atlantic. This huge mass of algae – about ten million tons – takes up a vast area of ocean, (around 7,000,000,000 square kilometres) – the Sargasso Sea, a threat to sailors for centuries, from the time of Christopher Columbus. Its tangled mass was thought to ensnare ships and the belief was that nobody could stay there without getting caught up in it.

22 What is plankton?

Plankton is a body of vegetable and animal beings which live in the sea.

They cannot usually move on their own, and even when they can, they do not have the strength to go against the currents, the tides or the winds which carry them along. Most of them are tiny.

Plankton form the first link of the chain of marine life, being the food for many sea creatures.

They live near the coast, where they can find the mineral salts and the light which they need to survive.

And because plankton is eaten by many fish, this explains why the coast is the best place for fishing, whereas the high sea is the worst.

Vegetable matter also forms part of plankton – numerous microscopic algae and animals, who live by grazing on the "pastures" of vegetable plankton. And as well as fish, there are many other eaters of plankton, such as sponges, corals, mussels and whales.

23 Do marine animals migrate?

Marine animals migrate in two ways – across water, and up and down.

Each evening, millions of sea creatures migrate from the bottom to the top, following the light of the sun until it disappears, then going down again with the light of a new day.

This natural instinct also makes lobsters, prawns and crabs descend into deep water to lay their eggs, and the marine spider to return to earth for the same reason.

Whales and tuna fish cross the oceans, seals and otters swim towards earth in February and March in hundreds of thousands.

Sharks and turtles migrate either alone or in groups.

Others, like the herring, mackerel and squid migrate in their thousands.

Many cover great distances – such as the Arctic Tern, who, in order to start a family within the Arctic Circle will fly around 20,000 kilometres from the Antarctic!

24 Are all sharks dangerous?

Usually, when we talk about sharks, we are thinking of the man-eaters, such as the White Shark.

But really, these ferocious creatures are only one type of shark, which in turn belong to a very large family of animals. The man-eating shark is the best known representative of this family, and justly deserves its reputation.

The star of many horror films, the man-eating shark is certainly a dangerous and aggressive animal with a huge appetite. It is often more than ten metres long with numerous lines of pointed teeth.

The White Shark is more common in Australian seas than anywhere else – whereas in Europe, it is the Blue Shark which is more common. And although this is a smaller type of shark, it is still best avoided!

In the North Atlantic, we meet the Sand Shark, always ready to attack, and very dangerous.

But the most dangerous of all sharks is the Tiger Shark – only four metres long, but fierce and always on the look-out for something to eat.

Then there is the Hammerhead Shark, with the courage to attack other sharks as well as humans.

The Whale Shark is the biggest living fish, up to twenty metres long. But it is harmless and peace-loving, feeding on plankton and living in tropical seas.

Only a little smaller is the Elephant Shark – so called because when it is young, it has a long muzzle, rather like an elephant's trunk. The Elephant Shark lives in the Northern Atlantic – and when it is young, it can also be found in the Mediterranean.

25 How many types of shells are there?

Shells are the outer skeletons of many sea creatures. They appeared on Earth a thousand, million years ago, and when Man arrived, there was already a vast assortment!

He used them as spoons, trays, bowls, wore them on string around his neck... and some, such as Cowrie shells, he used as money.

A collector of shells can never say "My collection is complete" – because nobody can say how many types of shells there are.

26 Are there insects which can go underwater?

There are fewer insects living in water than on land. Among them is the Pondskater, which "walks" on the water's surface, and the Water Boatman, which swims underwater, taking in air at the surface. The Lesser Water Boatman swims on its stomach on the surface, going under when it sees something to eat. Both the Water Scorpion, flat and oval-shaped, and the thin Water Stick Insect, have tubes through which they breathe.

27 What is an atoll?

Atolls are ring-shaped coral reefs which encircle a lagoon, of which the depth can vary between eighteen and seventy-five metres.

The word "atoll" comes from an expression in the Maldive language which means "lagoon island".

Coral is formed from millions of the hard skeletons of tiny sea creatures called polyps, pressed together, until they actually form mountains which eventually appear above the level of the sea.

Many of the reefs are between 300 – 500 metres up to 1,000 metres wide.

The diameter of the lagoon can vary, too, reaching widths of between 70 and 100 kilometres.

Charles Darwin, the British explorer and naturalist, believed that atolls began with a coral reef encircling an island which later disappeared into the ocean. But, because of the coral base, the circular reef grew again to the top, emerging above the waters of the sea, and bringing with it the sand and soil so that plants and trees then grew in the ring shape of the atoll.

This could be why almost all atolls seem to "rise up" in the sea, away from the coasts, particularly in the Pacific and Indian Oceans.

Certainly, everything which grows on an atoll is lush and green, especially the coconut palms.

These are those "coral islands" which people picture in their minds, with their white beaches, palms waving in the warm breezes, mirror-like waters and an ocean lost on the horizon under a clear, bright sky….. the perfect idea of paradise, and much admired by all who see them.

28 How do we get salt from the sea?

Man soon discovered the uses of salt – sodium chloride – in preserving and flavouring food. In the sea quantities vary from 20 to 40 kilogrammes per cubic metre.

The easiest way of getting salt from the sea is by evaporating the water in the sun and the wind.

To do this, a rainy and water-tight area is found near the sea, with salt extracted from lines of shallow tanks filled by sea water at high tide.

Then once the tanks are filled to a level of about 20 metres, the sluice gates controlling the flow of sea water into the tanks close.

The tide begins to retreat, and the sea water remaining in the tanks begins to evaporate in the sun and the wind, leaving salt on the bottom.

This salt will then be raked through and collected.

But as the climate for this operation is very important, these salt-works are only built where there is mostly sun and wind and very little rain.

29 Was there really a lost continent of Atlanta

There is an old legend about a great island, as big as Asia, which was situated off the Straits of Gibraltar – "outside the world", according to the Greek writer, Plato. He called it Atlanta, and said that it was once inhabited by fearless warriors who came close to conquering all Europe and Asia. But they were driven back by the Greeks and returned to Atlanta, which, in time, sank into the ocean.

Had the Ancient Greeks invented the whole thing? Or, is there some truth in this old story?

Certainly, on the sea beds there are mountain chains, together with the remains of animals and plants.

So many underwater explorers think that millions of years ago, Atlanta really did exist, a huge continent which, in the course of millions of years was swallowed up by the sea.

But, perhaps not all the continent sank. Greenland, the Azores off the coast of Portugal and the Canary Islands could be all that remains today.

30 What is archaeology of the sea about?

Archaeology is a science which studies ancient things, finding out their age and how they were used, to help us know more about how people lived in ancient times.

When a length of coastline has submerged under water, marine archaeologists often find vases, statues, etc. from houses which were once there.

They also find the remains of wrecked ships and their cargoes.

Archaeologists are interested in the ships themselves, finding out how they were built, and also what they carried.

Where they find a merchant ship, there will also be the stone jars which held wine, oils, honey, grain, cheese and fish – as well as money and precious objects. For hundreds of years these stone jars were containers for almost anything!

Ships also carried statues, materials, animals and plants.

One of the richest trading areas was the Mediterranean, because of the many ports along its coasts.

Archaeologists once used divers to bring things to the surface for them to see – and in 1907, off the coast of Tunisia, these divers recovered so many objects that they filled six rooms of a museum!

But today marine archaeologists have the equipment to do their own diving, so that they can see the objects first before moving them. In this way, they find out much more, and there is a better chance of recovering items intact. This is how whole ships have been re-built.

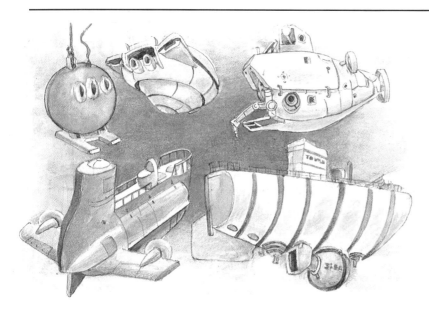

31 What is a bathysphere and a bathyscaph?

The bathysphere is a steel sphere with look-out windows, lowered underwater by a cable on a ship.

The bathyscaph is an underwater vehicle, an "ocean balloon" which can move freely, with a cockpit for the captain and space for a crew.

Both the bathysphere and the bathyscaph are means of studying the sea and sea bed. William Beebe reached the greatest depth in a bathysphere, descending 923 metres off the coast of Bermuda in 1934.

SAILING

Sir Francis Drake

Sir Francis Drake

ALMOST A YEAR had passed – and still the end of the voyage was not yet in sight.

From a fleet of five ships, only *The Golden Hind* remained. Many of the 176 men who had set sail now lay in the ocean.

Francis Drake sighed to himself as he sat quietly on deck in the shadow of the great sails.

Two sailors stopped nearby.

"Well," said the youngest, a boy of sixteen, "I think the worst is over."

"No, lad!" said the other, an older man with a patch over one eye. "With Captain Drake, the worst is over only when we drop anchor in an English port!"

"You're saying there's still more to come?" The boy could hardly believe his ears. "After we have gone through the Straits of Magellan without a single storm?"

"This is the coast of Chile!" the older sailor broke in. "Then there is Peru, both countries from which the Spanish take gold and silver, treasures for Philip of Spain – as Drake well remembers from the battles we have fought!"

"And I remember you, Jack of Tavistock!" came Drake's voice as he approached. "And the eye you lost, fighting with me!"

"Even so, Captain" said Jack, with a little bow. "And this is John, my nephew. He too comes from Tavistock, a Devon man like us!"

"And it is your first voyage?" Drake asked the boy. "We seafaring Devon men need to feel the ship's deck under our feet, with the sky above our heads. I have become rich, and Jack here keeps his family in comfort whilst we are out here, risking our lives!"

"I have bought a fine house," agreed Jack, "a farm, cattle, a workshop... But I cannot stay on land longer than a few months!"

"Uncle Jack says we may soon be attacking the Spanish," John interrupted, wanting to impress the great sea captain. "But there are only a few of us!"

Drake smiled at the boy.

"Yes," he said, "there are only a few of us. But they do not know we are here. Before us, only Magellan passed this way, so surprise will be our most powerful weapon! I believe we shall get a rich booty without too much

trouble!"

"Exactly so, Captain!" cried Jack. "The Spanish are usually ready for action in the Caribbean, not along this coast! How many times have we been attacked by them?"

"I was with Captain Drake when he commanded his first ship, the *Judith*," he told John proudly. "I was only twenty, or thereabouts, but I soon learned that we had to keep close on the heels of the Spanish fleet!"

"Don't believe him!" Drake broke in with a laugh. "At San Juan, the Spanish gave us a good

hiding, and when we got back to port, Jack said he would never go on a ship commanded by me again!"

"Not so!" cried Jack. "I said that after returning home from a voyage without an eye and with an empty pocket, I would be better off making lace with my wife!"

"Well, this time, I shall also bring back a fine gift to our Queen Elizabeth!" Drake's voice took on a note of pride which did not escape young John's notice.

"A gift for the Queen?" he repeated. "What gift is that

Captain Drake?"

"Maps of the spice routes!" Drake told him. "England will become more powerful with this voyage of ours, the first Englishmen to go round the world, flying our flag against the Spanish and the Portuguese and opening up new paths for our merchants!"

John could not speak. He had never imagined that he would one day be writing a piece of his country's history.

Under Francis Drake's command, his life as a seafarer would be full of adventure. This brave privateer would take him on many voyages during the years, along the routes to the East Indies and around the Cape of Good Hope, then back to Europe.

And there would be battles against the Spanish. Francis Drake would attack the armada of Philip of Spain at San Domingo, taking all their riches.

And John would be at the side of Captain Drake on the day when Queen Elizabeth would come on board *The Golden Hind* to make him a knight, and give him the title of Sir Francis Drake.

1 How did men sail in Prehistoric times?

Men soon realised that water could be used to carry cargoes along rivers, lakes and seas, keeping in sight of a coast. The first "boats" were simply trunks of trees, followed by hollowed-out trunks which they moved with rods or simply with the current, and then trunks tied together to make the first rafts. They also used inflated animal skins and basket-boats made with skins stretched around a framework of wood.

2 How did the Ancient Babylonians sail?

We know what ancient boats looked like from paintings – but also from the fact that some types are still used in many parts of the world.

In Mesopotamia, for example, along the rivers Tigris and Euphrates, the *kuffa* is still used today – a round boat, with skins stretched over a framework of wood. Moved along by poles or oars, the *kuffa* has been in use for thousands of years.

The amazing thing is that far from Mesopotamia, similar boats were being made! It seems that man found much the same ways of solving the same problems!

Very much like the *kuffa* is the coracle, still being used in Wales and parts of Ireland.

The *kuffa* is only one of many Mesopotamian boats.

There were also many types of canoes and rafts made with bunches of rushes tied together.

Then they found a way of sailing with a sail. Evidence of the first sailing ship dates back about 6,000 years.

3 How did the Ancient Egyptians build their boats?

The Ancient Egyptians built boats of wood, but mostly papyrus, a plant which grew abundantly in their country.

They made big strips of papyrus stems and tied them together to make boats which were a cross between the tree trunk and a raft, moved first by poles and paddles, then by a sail, as well.

Similar boats are still used today, 1,000 kilometres away, on Lake Titicaca in South America.

4 How was a trireme built?

Apart from the cargo ships in ancient times, there had to be war-ships. The first were rather flat and stocky, so that they could carry lots of cargo. But those which came later had to be fast, so they had a more tapering shape. Both had sails and rudders, but the war-ship could not afford to trust the wind completely. So, they were equipped with rows or banks of oars, which could also be used to turn the ship quickly.

Greek warriors probably went to Troy in galleys – ships with one bank of oars. Phoenicians, Etruscans, then the Greeks made two banks of oars to make the fast-moving Bireme. The Greeks perfected this with the Trireme, a ship with three banks of oars, heavier than a Bireme but able to attack with more force. In 430 B.C. at Salamina, 310 Greek Triremes commanded by Temistocles destroyed 1207 Persian ships which were bigger and with higher sides – but which could not move so easily in the water.

5 How big were caravels?

Caravels were Portuguese fishing and coastal sailing ships which appeared in the Mediterranean in the 14th Century. They were widely used in the exploration of the sea.

The fleet of Christopher Columbus consisted of two caravels, the Pinta and the Nina, and a carrack, the Santa Maria – a ship we cannot date so easily.

The Pinta, commanded by Martin Alonso Pinzon and with a crew of 25 men, had square sails. It was about 18 – 23 metres long, and between 5 – 7.5 metres wide.

The Nina had triangular sails. It was 21 metres long and 6 metres wide, with a crew of 20 men.

The Santa Maria was commanded by Columbus – although he preferred the Nina because of the way she could be handled in the water.

The Santa Maria was 23.70 metres long, 7.2 metre wide and with 39 men on board

Unfortunately, the Santa Maria was wrecked on the night of 24th December 1492, off the coast of Hispaniola, now known as Haiti.

6 How do a privateer and pirate differ?

A privateer was a navigator, authorised by a monarch's letter, which was carried on to enemy ships as a warrant to seize goods. At the time of Elizabeth I, the privateers' war centred on spices - one aspect of the war between Spain and England. The most famous were Hawkins, Raleigh and Drake.

Pirates worked in the same way – but because they had no letter of authority, they were acting against the law!

7 How far did the Vikings reach?

The Ancient Vikings saw that the wild geese flew each year from the north direct to the west, across the Atlantic Ocean. This told them that the geese must find land, so they decided to leave their fjords and set sail across the ocean.

Even in prehistoric times, they explored the whole of the Scandinavian coast up to the extreme north, as well as the coasts of the Baltic Sea and the North Sea.

They sailed up Russian rivers, linking the Baltic and the Black Sea, and developing trade with the rich Byzantine Empire. They navigated western European rivers, the English, French and Spanish coasts, and conquered parts of England, France and Sicily.

Between the 9th and the 15th Century, the Vikings set their sights further to the North West, reaching Iceland, Greenland, Labrador and Newfoundland – and so arriving in America centuries before Christopher Columbus!

8 How was the first submersible made?

A submarine is a ship built to move underwater. But a submersible is a craft which can only go underwater for short periods.

The first true submersibles were built by two Americans – David Bushnell and Robert Fulton at the end of the 17th century.

Fulton's submersible had a wooden hull similar to an ordinary boat, a propeller, look-out tower, and two sails. He called it *Nautilus*.

9 How does a nuclear submarine work?

Before the nuclear submarine, underwater vehicles were powered by battery-driven electric motors – which meant surfacing every so often to get the batteries charged. But motors powered by a nuclear reactor meant the submarine could move underwater much more quickly and be quite independent. This was when the true submarine was born.

The first nuclear powered submarine was launched in the United States in 1955, and was called the *Nautilus* – after the vessel in Jules Verne's story *2,000 Leagues Under the Sea* which described the adventures of an underwater boat with a system of propulsion quite different to anything known before, powerful and inexhaustible – the nuclear submarine.

The *Nautilus* of 1955 covered 1,300 miles underwater on its first voyage, driven for eighty and a quarter days. The first charge of power from the reactor was exhausted after 26 months and almost 70,000 miles.

10 How can a person survive a shipwreck?

The main dangers of being ship-wrecked are dehydration – drying out of the body – and thirst. Sea water gives only temporary relief.

On 24th August 1952, to show it was possible to survive at sea without food or water, French doctor, Alain Bombard, left Casablanca off the coast of Morocco in a dinghy with a sail, but no radio, food or drink.

He ate only raw fish and plankton, drinking every three to four days the few drops of water which had collected on the ship. In between, he drank sea water – no more than a litre a day.

On 23rd December, he arrived at the Canary Islands, 20 kilogrammes lighter and having suffered only from the heat and stomach upsets!

To avoid dehydration, people are told to avoid sweating too much, alcohol and exposure to the sun, and to wash clothes every day. Sugar lumps, sweets or candied fruit are all good for quenching thirst.

11 Are solo sea-crossings a recent happening?

The first recorded solo sea-crossing was in 1601 by a Dutch doctor Henri De Voogt, rowing from Holland to London.

In the 19th century, there began a series of solo crossings, the first by the American Crenston, who in 1849 sailed from New Bedford to San Francisco, rounding Cape Horn.

The first Atlantic crossing was by Alfred Johnson. He commemorated the Independence of the United States by sailing to Nova Scotia from Wales. The first to go around the world following the route of Magellan was the Canadian Joshua Slocum in 1895. And the youngest round-the-world sailor was American Lee Graham, who set off in 1965 at the age of seventeen.

And the strongest? He was an Italian who in 1923 fled from prison in Guyana and reached Europe in a canoe! Sailing to Guyana from Africa in 1937, a Dutchman, Kuyt, put cold compresses on the forehead of a seriously ill companion, and saved his life.

Norwegian Al Hansen took his dog when he sailed around Cape Horn against the current in 1928, and, with his eight-year-old daughter, Spaniard Henry Blanco sailed from Barcelona to Tahiti in 1931.

Most famous was Francis Chichester who left Plymouth, England, in 1966, rounding Cape Horn and returning by the course taken by the old tea clipper ships. For this achievement, Queen Elizabeth knighted him with the same sword Queen Elizabeth I had used for Sir Francis Drake.

12 How do ships enter harbour?

All ships need help to enter and then weigh anchor in harbour. This help comes from a tug-boat, or small ship, which has the job of steering larger ships in and out.

Their help is also necessary because there may be obstacles, sudden depths and other dangers which the commander of a ship may not know about, and which could cause difficulties.

So, by following the little tug, the big ship can move safely.

13 What is the use of buoys?

Buoys are floating objects of various types and which are anchored in the sea. Some buoys have a bell, which, with the movement of the waves, gives a danger signal when there is a sea mist.

Then there is a luminous buoy, which gives light to signal danger at night and a mooring buoy, with a chain on which a ship can anchor.

And in the case of accident, a ship can disconnect a buoy's radio so that it sends out a continuous alarm call.

Buoys are also used in regattas to set out the course which competitors have to follow. At the start and at the finish, there is a buoy with a black and white checked flag – and before each of these, a buoy with a flag of red and white squares.

The buoy around which competitors have to turn has a yellow flag, a buoy signifying danger a red flag, and a buoy showing the way to follow, a white flag.

14 Hovercraft, seaplane, hydrofoil – what are they?

The hovercraft is rather like a huge rubber dinghy which moves just a few centimetres above the water on a cushion of air generated by a "blower". It can travel over land, too.

The hovercraft was invented in 1954 by Sir Christopher Cockerell. Over fifty are now in service.

The seaplane is an aircraft designed to land and take off on water – but not on dry land. It is mostly in disuse nowadays. So, the seaplane is an aircraft which goes on water – and the hydrofoil is a boat which can fly!

It has wings – so, when it reaches a certain speed in water, it takes off, rising just above the water and travelling at high speed.

It was invented by Italian engineer Enrico Forlanini in 1903, and came to be used as a method of public transport in later years.

Today, hydrofoils are still used on seas and inland lakes because they are much faster than ships and do not need a runway to land.

15 What is surfing?

Surfing is a sport where people ride the waves, balanced on a board 2.5 metres long. It needs long, ocean waves, so it is most popular in Australia, South Africa and the United States.

It began in Hawaii as a religious ritual, where people saw in the great waves the strength and power of the ocean gods.

To challenge and control this power of the ocean gods was thought to be proof of courage and skill.

16 What is a regatta?

Regattas are races between sailing clubs and schools. They began in Venice as a way of training young sailors for war, with the first regatta there recorded as 25th January 1315.

This first regatta is still commemorated on the first Sunday in September, with a regatta in Venice. This is the most famous of all historical regattas, with oarsmen dressed in period costume, held to celebrate a special event.

The famous Transatlantic Race or Regatta was started in 1866, when three yacht owners challenged each other to cross the Atlantic for a prize of one million dollars, put up by an American. It was won by James Gordon Bennet on his yacht Henrietta. The regatta began to be officially organised in 1905. The most famous water speed trophy is the America's Cup, open to challenge by the fastest racing yachts of any nation. Yachting teams from the United States have won the Cup the most times.

17 What is an outboard motor?

Some motor-boats are powered by an outboard motor, fitted outside the craft, and some boats have the engine inside.

Other motor-boats have an internal outboard motor, which is a motor actually on board the boat, rather than being outside, but the motion is transmitted to a propeller – so the motor is half inside, and half outside. The internal outboard motor is most popular, used in motorboats for leisure as well as for racing.

18 How were sea battles once fought?

There was a time when warships faced each other directly. Cannons and battering rams made up much of naval warfare in those days.

Before the appearance of fire-arms, sailors would try to ram an opposing ship, then invade and conquer it.

But when fire-arms came on the scene, ships had the power to fire at enemies from a distance. Then they could board them by force.

19 How is an aircraft carrier made?

At the end of the First World War, bigger ships began being modified to provide enough space for aircraft to take off and land. These were the first aircraft carriers, which changed the method of sea warfare completely, taking the place of the mighty battleships.

For aircraft to take off and land, an aircraft carrier needs a huge and completely clear deck, which is level on all sides.

The deck is divided into three parts – the landing deck, where the aircraft must land; the middle zone, where the aircraft waits to take off; and the fore deck.

The aeroplanes are kept under the deck in enormous hangars, with huge lifts taking them up to the deck. So the aircraft carrier is, in fact, a type of airport at sea.

The biggest and most powerful aircraft carriers are those for attack; smaller and less powerful are those for escort, although these can still have the task of defending an attack by submarines.

20 What happens today in naval battles?

The aircraft carrier has entirely changed the style of war at sea.

At the start of the Second World War, ships no longer had to rely on head-on confrontation to attack enemy ships. Instead, they could embark with aircraft carriers to strike at the enemy and to defend them. With look-out aircraft and Radar to identify the enemy, some aircraft would go into the attack and others defend ships from other enemy aircraft.

21 What made the Titanic sink?

In Spring the temperature rises, and the Ice Pack, the blanket of ice covering the North and South Poles, breaks along the edges. Then, huge icebergs break loose and drift with the current.

On the night of 14th – 15th April 1912, whilst sailing to New York, the great British liner Titanic hit an iceberg which made an enormous hole.

In less than three hours, the ship had sunk with the loss of 1,500 lives.

22 How do ships float?

We do not wonder how a tree trunk can float – because we know that wood is lighter than water.

But, steel is heavier than water. A bolt or nail will sink. So, how can a ship with a steel hull float?

Let us imagine a 10cms steel cube, weighing 7.85 kilogrammes.

If we could weigh it in water, its weight would be 6.85 kilogrammes – one kilogramme less.

What has happened is that the 10cm cube has displaced 10cm cubed of water, equal to one litre.

So, a litre of water has the same volume as a 10cm cube – which means the cube gets an upward "push", equal to the weight of the water it has moved, or displaced – and as a litre weighs a kilo, that is the kilo difference in weight which we noted at the beginning.

A cube of steel does not float, because the water cannot support it. But, if we could melt down the cube and make it into a little boat, we would still have the same weight – but it would be spread out to make a greater "mass". The boat would displace much more water than the cube. Placed in 7.85 litres of water, it gets an upward thrust equal to 7.85 kilogrammes – and so, it floats!

Try putting a small saucepan in a bowl of water, and see how the level of the water rises.Then load and unload it with pebbles. See the saucepan sinking or rising up, according to the amount of water it displaces and the relative "push" which it gets!

23 How do you sail against the wind?

The path a sailing ship can take depends on the direction of the wind. If the wind blows from behind, that is to stern, or a "following wind", the sails fill out and the ship can speed on ahead. Also if the wind blows on the side, that is a "beam wind", the ship can sail straight ahead.

But if the wind comes from the front, a "head wind", the ship cannot go straight ahead.

Instead the sailor has to catch the wind, so that the ship can move on, still following its proper course.

Otherwise, the ship is at the mercy of the current, going only wherever the wind blows it.

So, the yachtsman has to follow a zig-zag route, turning the ship first one way and then the other to catch the wind in the sails, going from port to starboard, starboard to port.

Using the sails in this way, it is possible to sail against the wind.

Going forward in a zig-zag manner like this is called "tacking" – probably because the sailor "tacks" on to one end and then the other alternately.

24 What is a catamaran?

The word catamaran comes from the language of the Tamil people who live in Southern India and the island of Sri Lanka. It means "tied wood" and comes from a type of primitive raft of ancient times consisting of no more than a tree-trunk tied in such a way that the centre dips in the centre.

A catamaran is driven by oars and sometimes by a sail – in which case, it is sometimes called a "calamarina".

It is a craft which is typical of the Indian and Sri Lankan coast – but, as with all ancient crafts, it is found in other parts of the world, such as Australia, Tasmania and Polynesia.

The modern catamaran used in sport is made up of two floats joined by a bridge. A mast for the sail is mounted in the centre of the bridge.

A specially-built catamaran can be used to carry passengers – as the Japanese have shown, launching a passenger service in 1965 and carrying at least 320 people between Hiroshima and Shikoku.

25 How does a compass work?

A compass is an instrument in a container which gives an exact direction. It has a magnetic needle pivoted to swing within a circle of 360 degrees, so that it will always point towards north. This reference to north and the helmsman's "line of sight" to the horizon, gives a "heading" – a fixed direction in line with the prow of the ship.

This heading is then taken by degrees along the route to follow.

26 How can ships find their way?

Many people call this "orientating" which comes from the word "orient" meaning east – because maps were once drawn with the east at the top instead of the north, as they are today. But it is perhaps more commonly known as "navigation".

Finding the way, or navigating with a compass is easy, because it always points to the north.

If, for example, we wanted to go east, we would only need to find north to our right. Otherwise, we could look at the sun. At six o'clock in the morning, the sun is in the east. At noon, it is in the south and at six o'clock in the evening, in the West. So, to go east, we would simply go in the direction in which the sun rises!

More precise is the method using a clock. Point the hour hand in the direction of the sun, then put a small stick at twelve on the dial. The angle between the hour hand and the stick indicates south.

By night, we could use the stars, just as ancient seamen did! Find in the night sky the constellation of Ursa Major (The Plough). Look for the two lowest stars in this constellation and imagine them joining in a line. Continue this line five times the same distance and you will see the Pole Star, which indicates north.

Because the sky is not always the same, we can only use the Pole Star in spring and summer. In autumn and winter we have to use the constellation of Orion. But, this is more complicated – and when the weather gets colder, perhaps it is best to stay at home....

27 How does an echo-sounder work?

An echo-sounder is an instrument which explores the sea using echoes.

An acoustic, or ultrasound signal is sent underwater by a ship, and this "bounces off" the sea bed or an obstacle before returning. The time taken between the sound being sent and returning indicates the depth. A series of continual sounds is sent from the ship and so the echoes return in a series. In this way, it is possible to trace the course of the sea bed or the size of an obstacle and this is then "drawn" on a screen, making it visible as well as audible.

An echo-sounder can also be used when a ship is going at high speed.

The idea of getting information by sending sounds which then bounce back comes from bats. These animals are blind, but they have highly sensitive hearing and fly around using the echoes of ultrasounds which they make themselves. So, although the echo-sounder was invented by man, nature was already using the idea!

28 How is a nautical chart made?

Nautical charts are special maps on which we find marked an outline of the coasts, important coastal points, maritime signals – buoys, pylons, etc. – sea depths, the type of sea bed and currents.

All this is necessary for navigation and the charts are compiled by special institutes.

There are two types of nautical charts – those for coastal navigation and the high seas and those for ocean navigation.

Nautical charts began in ancient times. They were already in use during the Greek-Roman Empire, quickly spreading throughout the Middle East, and showing all the ancient ports. The oldest example is Italian and dates from the beginning of the 14th century.

Nautical charts today are published with photographs and drawings, being constantly up-dated by marine experts. These charts are absolutely necessary in sailing and ships big and small are supplied with them.

29 What is a container ship?

Not so long ago, if a factory making bolts had to send some overseas, they had to pack the bolts, put the packs on a lorry, which took them to a port.

Once there, the packs had to be unloaded, then loaded again on to the ship.

On arrival, the whole operation had to be repeated, in reverse. There was always the chance of containers breaking, bolts coming out, a container remaining on the lorry and goods getting mixed up on the ship.

But in recent years, factories have been loading goods into a huge metal container, which is loaded by crane on to a lorry, then driven to port.

There, another crane takes the container and loads it straight on to the ship. And on arrival, the same thing happens, in reverse. The risk of damage is reduced and also the time taken in loading and unloading. Every type of merchandise can be carried by a container ship, and the advantages are enormous.

30 What is a sextant?

Calculating the position of a ship is a problem which sailors have always had.

The first instrument to help was an astrolabe and one example was found on the wreck of a 14th century Greek ship. This developed into the sextant, which is shaped like a sixth of a circle – "sesto " in Italian, from which the sextant gets its name – with a little telescope and two mirrors, one fixed, the other movable.

The telescope is pointed towards the sun, then the movable mirror turned until the sun is reflected in it.

Once the navigator gets the image of the sun's reflection, so that it appears to "sit" on the horizon, the navigator checks by how many degrees he has had to move the sextant arm. Using this measurement with the height of the sun, the navigator can work out how many degrees north or south of the equator the ship is. For night-time navigation, the North Star is normally used.

THE SKY

An Eclipse of The Sun

An Eclipse Of The Sun

CONSTANTINE WAS TIRED of eating only goats' cheese, olives and dry figs!

The rainy summer meant that the bees had been unable to make much honey. Now there was none left to make even one biscuit – and it seemed the winter would never end.

But at least, he thought, the wild cherries growing around the fields nearby showed signs of ripening at last. The sun was warm and bright, not hiding behind the rain-clouds as it had last year..... and Mount Immitos, where he took the sheep to pasture, was green, the air scented with myrtle.

Constantine was twelve years old. He had lived at the monastery since he was three. His father had been one of the heroes in defence of Constantinople when the Turks had besieged the city.

His mother had managed to give her little son into the care of an old monk for safety, and he had brought the baby to the monastery in Athens.

Since then, the boy had wanted for nothing, never knowing hunger nor cold. And he was tutored by Demetrius, known throughout the area as a most wise, clever monk, whilst Brother Basil taught him about plants and maps.

But Constantine had been a sad, lonely boy – until a monk from another monastery chanced to call.

"Tell me," he said, as he and the other monks spoke together, "could there have been a boy brought here after the siege of Constantinople?"

To everyone's joy, Constantine heard that his parents were alive and living in Corinth, after searching for him in all the monasteries throughout Greece!

How the good monks celebrated such wonderful news!

Afterwards, it was decided that it would be best for Constantine to stay at the monastery for a few years longer to finish his education. But his mother and father often came to see the son they both thought they had lost.

From then on, the unhappy child changed.

He ran, he jumped, he played, running after the sheep and goats and with the monks threatening

all kinds of punishment when he was naughty – but it was no good!

Now in such high spirits, Constantine began to tire of the monastery, seeing only the monks and eating plain food all the time.

It seemed to be a place where nothing exciting happened...

Just then, Constantine noticed that there seemed to be a lot of chatter going on, making the monastery much noisier and more bustling than usual.

Brother Michael, the cook, was looking up at the sky, getting so worked up about something, he

had spilt a barrel of olives!

Brother Basil's eyes were also on the sky and so many monks were asking Brother Demetrius questions, he was already looking quite weary.

Constantine did not take much notice. He was dreaming of having a feed of cherries and going home to Corinth in a few days.

That night, he and Demetrius were the only ones who slept soundly. The other monks whispered and murmured amongst themselves – and by the next morning, they seemed so

uneasy and restless.

And, Constantine? He was looking forward to eating a few cherries when he took the sheep to graze!

"No, Constantine!" came the voice of Demetrius. "Don't go out! Leave the sheep for now!"

And off he hurried towards his cell! Constantine could not understand it.

And – why was it becoming dark? Surely, no cloud was big enough to hide the sun completely?

Constantine shaded his eyes, watching it becoming black.... Sheep began bleating in fright, hens squawked and cats ran inside.

He could not help giving a cry of alarm, his heart thumping.

Then came a firm hand on his shoulder. "I am sorry, Constantine," came the calm voice of Brother Demetrius. "I had forgotten you did not know about an eclipse of the sun. Do not be afraid of this darkness. You will soon see the sun again."

Constantine did not answer. By now, it was completely dark.

"Look well," said Brother Demetrius. "Later, I shall tell you all about an eclipse of the sun."

May

1 What is a climate?

The climate is the whole range of weather conditions found in a region or area during the course of a year.

The elements which make up the climate are – temperature, winds, atmospheric pressure (measured by barometer), humidity and rainfall.

We also take into account the geographic features which have a bearing on these elements – such as latitude, distance from the sea and exposure to the sun.

2 How do we classify climates?

There are five main climates. The tropical climate is rainy, with no cold seasons – moist-damp rain forests and savannah jungle areas.

The dry, arid (or parched) desert climate, includes the semi-arid climate of the steppes, the plains of Asia.

The temperate climate brings mainly dry winters and summers in the Mediterranean and cold, damp winters further north.

The glacial climate extends across the Tundra – the frozen Arctic desert, and other icy regions. The climate is a big influence on health. Infectious diseases spread rapidly in warm countries, whereas in cold climates, more people suffer with complaints like rheumatism and lung diseases. The warm, sea climate with its pure air, rich in iodine and salt, helps those suffering from asthma and breathlessness And dry, mountain air is rich in the essence of balsam – wonderful for anaemia, exhaustion or people recovering from illness.

3 What is a rainbow?

A rainbow is seen when it is raining and sunny at the same time.

When it rains, the rays of the sun hit the raindrops, splitting them into seven colours and bending them as it passes through to form an arch of coloured light. From the outside (or east), the colours are – red, orange, yellow, green, blue, indigo and violet.

As for the gold at the end of the rainbow, nobody's found it yet!

4 What is a drought?

Drought is a lack or scarcity of rain which goes on for an unusually long time.

The rainfall of a region or locality is calculated on the amount of rain which falls during a year – including the number of days with rainfall of a certain type – rain, snow and hail.

With each region having its own records of rainfall, people can measure if and when this is scarce enough to become a drought.

5 What is wind?

The wind is a horizontal movement of a mass of air caused by variations in pressure.

The Beaufort Scale classifies wind from 1 – 12 degrees, based on wind-speed. Force 0, with a speed of less than 1 kilometre an hour, is absolute calm. Force 1, a puff of wind, has a speed of 1 – 5 kilometres an hour, enough to bend a column of smoke or steam. Force 2 is a light breeze from 7 – 11 kilometres an hour, moving leaves. Force 3, a stiff breeze, blows at between 12 – 19 kilometres an hour, rustling leaves and moving weather-cocks. Force 4, a moderate wind between 20 – 28 kilometres an hour, will spin weather-cocks and make small trees move.

Force 5, a stiff wind with a speed of between 29 – 38 kilometres per hour, will move big branches of trees and make waters swell. And Force 6, a fresh wind between 39 – 49 kilometres per hour, can be heard indoors. Force 7, a strong wind of between 50 – 71 kilometres per hour, is hard to walk against. Force 8 is storm force, 72 – 74 kilometres per hour, able to break branches and move big trees! Force 9, a strong gale, between 75 – 88 kilometres per hour, sends roof-tiles flying.

Force 10, strongest gale, 89 – 102 kilometres per hour, uproots trees. Force 11, hurricane winds with speeds of 103 – 117 kilometres per hour, bring about great disasters.

Then there is the Force 12 hurricane, blowing up to 120 kilometres an hour, causing terrible destruction.

6 What are breezes?

Breezes are light winds, maximum Force 3, caused by differences in temperature between the sea and land. Both become warm and cold at different speeds – slowly for the sea, quickly for the land.

By day, the air over the land rises up, and in its place comes the fresh air from above the sea. At sunset, the land is cool; so, the air above it is drawn to the sea, where the warmer air rises, making room for the cool air.

7 What are seasonal and constant winds?

"Seasonal" winds change their direction at different times – such as breezes and monsoons.

Monsoons are like enormous breezes. They blow up between oceans and continents and have whole seasons to themselves.

In the Indian Ocean, the monsoons blow from the north-east in winter – from continent to ocean (earth monsoons), and from the south-west in summer – from ocean to continent (sea monsoons).

The result of this change of direction is the succession of periods of rain and drought.

Constant or permanent winds are those which blow throughout the year in the same direction. We call them trade winds and they blow from the Tropic of Cancer and from the Tropic of Capricorn, towards the equator.

These are the winds which helped European navigators to reach Central America – including Christopher Columbus in the summer of 1492. It is very important for sailors to know wind speed and direction.

8 Why is the sky blue?

How is it that we see the sky as being blue, when air is colourless?

It is because of the dust in the air. The light of the sun shines through the dust, which acts as a filter, allowing only blue rays of light to rise above.

But when the air is polluted with too much harmful dust, this filters the rays more than needed and the sky is no longer blue. And where pollution reaches high levels, a blue sky is only a memory.

9 What are clouds?

Clouds are masses of drops of water or tiny ice crystals, formed when water vapour in the air liquifies.

Low clouds are those around 2400 metres above the earth, medium 2400 – 6000 metres and high up to 12,000 metres above the Earth.

High clouds are cirrus, cirro-stratus and cirro-cumulus, all made up of ice crystals. White or pink, the cirrus and cirro-stratus appear rather like threads or bits of wool, and the cirro-cumulus like a flock of sheep. Medium clouds, alto-cumulus and alto-stratus, made up of drops of water, are grey, round or sail-shaped, and always in groups.

Low clouds are strato-cumulus, round and dark, mostly seen in winter; stratus a dense layer of dark cloud, making the sky grey; and nimbo-stratus, dark and heavy, bringing rain or snow.

Then there are clouds which form vertically; the cauliflower-shaped cumulus, often seen on very hot days, and the cumulo-nimbus, dark with white edges, brings storms.

10 Why does it rain?

It rains, because the amount of water vapour in a cloud cools and changes into drops, which become too heavy for it to hold and so they fall to earth.

This happens in clouds of a certain thickness or which have a vertical rather than a horizontal shape, where the smallest drops are pushed up to the top, leaving the biggest to collect in the base of the cloud, until they become heavy enough to fall as rain.

Usually, drops of rain can measure anything up to three millimetres in diameter, although there have been some "monsters" between seven and eight millimetres.

Small raindrops fall slowly in a light drizzle which often it seems as if the rain is held in the air!

Sometimes in summer, there are cloudbursts, sudden, heavy falls of rain which fall with hardly any warning, often with strong winds, sometimes hail-stones. And the raindrops in a cloudburst are biggest of all! These showers of rain will usually stop just as suddenly as they began.

11 What is a mist?

A mist is exactly the same as a cloud, except that it is formed on the ground.

Mists arise when warm air passes above a cold surface, or when the lower layers of damp air become cold – for example, in contact with the ground.

In industrial areas, drops of water vapour condense (turn into liquid) around impurities and smoke particles, then a grey mist forms which people call "smog".

Mist is very changeable. It can form when the temperature drops by two or three degrees. And when it rises by the same amount, a mist can disappear.

The intensity of a mist can be measured by the visibility within it.

Less than 1 kilometre, the mist is thin. Less than 200 metres, the mist is thick.

Mist is a danger to all forms of transport.

When it is thick and persistent, ships have to use signalling equipment and airports are often closed.

12 How is dew formed?

On calm nights, as the ground cools down, it also cools the air around it. The water vapour in the air turns into tiny particles of water and these fall over everything.

Plants also give off water vapour – so where the water vapour in the air combines with that from plants, bigger drops are formed on leaves, flowers and grass, than those which fall on the ground – so, in the morning, we see the ground wet and drops of water on plants, as if it has been raining.

When the temperature falls below zero, they freeze into the little white grains or crystals of frost.

On damp and very cold nights, the frost and dew become ice which covers everything. This covering, giving a sparkling, fairy-tale look to our surroundings, is called hoar.

Frost and hoar frost are a danger to farmers and growers. If either occurs early in autumn or late in spring, they can endanger the flowering and so threaten the harvest later on in the year.

13 How do we get hail?

When particles of sleet form at a great height, they then fall through clouds carrying drops of rain. So, the sleet particles are enlarged by the rain gathering around each one and freezing.

Or, water drops in a cloud are carried up high into zones where the lower temperatures freeze them.

Hailstones – the balls of ice which fall – can be as small as a pea, or as large as an orange!

14 Where does snow come from?

We notice activity in the air only when there is a result we can see – wind, rain, frost and so on.

But lots has been happening before we see anything at all!

A snowflake begins as a single drop of water, suspended in the air at low altitude. Then, a current of air lifts it higher, and, as it rises, the water particle meets other water particles and gets bigger.

Still it rises, until it reaches the zones where the temperature is very low, and freezes into a five-sided crystal of ice.

Still, the crystal rises and collects more water which also freezes, making the crystal so heavy that it begins to fall towards the earth.

And as it falls, so it collects still more water vapour, becoming still bigger.

Sometimes, it will join with other crystals to make a snowflake – which, once it "lands" on earth, can melt or accumulate with other snowflakes, according to the temperature at the time.

And above certain altitudes, there is always snow – because it always accumulates, never melts.

The limit above which snow accumulates is called the boundary of perpetual snow and varies according to the latitude.

In the polar regions, the boundary of perpetual snow is situated at sea level.

In the Alps, it is around 3,000 metres; but, on the equator the altitude limit is around 4,000 metres.

15 What is lightning?

In the air, there are millions of particles with positive and negative electrical charges.

When the big storm clouds gather, the charged particles become more numerous and concentrated, becoming stronger and stronger, until a spark shoots across the space in between – lightning!

Lightning can happen within a cloud, between two different clouds and also between a cloud and the ground.

16 What is the Ozone Layer?

Ozone is a blue coloured gas which smells like garlic. It is present in the oxygen in the air following thunderstorms, near big electrical machines when they are working, and especially high up in the atmosphere.

Ozone is a powerful oxidiser which can rust all metals except platinum and gold.

It is also a disinfectant, germicide, deodorant and bleach, and one of its most important uses is the sterilisation of drinking water and swimming baths.

Other uses include preserving food, whitening paper and sugar and the preparation of perfumes and medicines.

Around 20 kilometres above Earth is the Ozone Layer which blocks out the harmful ultra-violet rays of the sun.

If this layer is reduced or punctured, these rays can heat up the Earth, causing variations in climate, skin diseases, and changes in the growth of plants and the supply of plankton on which fish feed.

17 What is "the greenhouse effect"?

The Earth is warmed by the sun and in return gives out heat into space. This "exchange" happens in the atmosphere, allowing the rays of the sun to pass and the Earth's heat to return from its source. If the atmosphere is polluted, the rays of the sun can pass, but because the Earth cannot return enough heat through the atmosphere, the balance between heat coming and heat going is altered and the Earth's temperature increases.

18 What is a falling star?

Falling "stars" are not stars at all! They are little stones which come from outer space, becoming white hot as they enter the Earth's atmosphere.

If they are not on fire, they will be difficult to see – they only weigh three quarters of a kilogram at most!

Are falling stars unusual? Not at all. It is estimated that each day at least 24 million enter the atmosphere – enough for 24 million wishes!

19 How does the moon change each month?

The sun, the Earth and the moon all move in space – which means we see different parts of the moon, and this, too, changes position in relation to the sun. The time that the moon takes to show itself to the "Earth-bound" is called a lunar month, lasting around 29 days and in which there are four phases of the moon.

Let us call day "zero" the time when we can hardly see the moon, because it is covered by the sun. This is the phase of the new moon.

From "day zero" to the seventh day, the moon gradually "waxes" (increases) from a crescent to a half moon. This continues until, by day fourteen, the moon is full.

Then the moon "wanes" – gets less and less until the 21st day, when all we see is a half moon – the opposite half to when the moon was growing. And in the next seven days, the moon becomes less and less visible, until on the 29th day, the moon's cycle is finished, ready to begin all over again.

20 Which planets can you see with the naked eye?

We can see Mercury, Venus, Mars, Jupiter and Saturn. Mercury is very near the sun. Visible at sunset and dawn, it is swathed in a dense atmosphere. Mars has ice-caps similar to those on Earth and canals furrowing its surface.

Jupiter, the giant of the Solar System, is picked out by red and yellow stripes and a big red blot. Most of us know Saturn because of its rings – but these cannot be seen with the naked eye.

21 What did ancient men see in the stars?

Among the millions of stars in the sky were many which fired the imagination of ancient man. To them, it seemed they made up certain shapes or formations – objects, animals, people. Among the observers of the sky were the Ancient Greeks who gave names to these figures, and made up stories about them. Nowadays, these figures – or constellations – are helpful to us in getting to know our way around the sky, and so their ancient myths have been handed down to us.

A few names? Andromeda. The Eagle. The Swan. The Dolphin. Ursa Major (The Great Bear, or Plough), Ursa Minor, (The Little Bear).

Then there is Orion, one of the most beautiful constellations. To the Ancient Greeks, Orion was the hunter who loved Eos, (Romans called her Aurora), goddess of the dawn. Artemis (or Diana) wounded him with a Scorpion sting and he became a constellation – the most easily seen during the winter months in Europe.

22 What is a comet?

The artist Giotto was one of many who painted scenes of the Nativity of Christ. The Bible says that a star stopped above the stable where Christ was born. But Giotto had seen something of what is now known as Halley's Comet – and he was not so convinced.

So, he painted a "star" quite different to anything seen before in pictures – a globe of light, with a tail.

For a long time, it was believed that comets were signs from the sky to show something was about to happen. In fact, they are heavenly bodies which go around the sun in an elliptical (oval shaped) orbit. So, they only appear at intervals – Halley's Comet, for example, returns every 77 years.

When comets pass near the sun, they take on the form by which we know them. Only the head of the comet is near to the sun – a bright nucleus globe surrounded by a soft haziness and tapering off into a long, shining tail.

23 What is the difference between planets and satellites?

Planets are heavenly bodies which orbit (travel around) the sun. They do not have their own light, but reflect light from the sun.

Satellites are also heavenly bodies, but much smaller than planets, which they orbit in the same way as planets orbit the sun. Satellites, too, reflect light from the sun. Except for Mercury and Venus, all planets have satellites. Earth's satellite is the moon.

24 How can we study the sky?

The first thing used to study the sky was the human eye! Then came the telescope – first used in astronomy by Galileo.

But telescope users had the problem of seeing coloured halos around the bright heavenly bodies until Sir Isaac Newton invented the rigid telescope, which became the basis of astronomy.

Nowadays, telescopes can be equipped with cameras! This means that astronomers can point the telescope towards a particular section of the sky which they want to observe, then leave it for the photographic plates to take pictures!

Because heavenly bodies give off radiation, radio telescopes were designed in order to study the radio waves given off into space by picking up the sounds – similar to the sounds which radio and televisions make when they pick up electrical charges during a storm.

This is how we can hear the sounds of Jupiter, Orion – even Halley's Comet, as it gets nearer!

1957 saw a number of big advances in astronomy.

The first radio telescope was used at England's Jodrell Bank and Russia launched Sputnik, the first artificial satellite.

Like natural satellites, these artificial satellites remain in space, going around a heavenly body.

After satellites were launched into orbit around Earth, many others were launched around other heavenly bodies, enabling astronomers to obtain lots more information.

With the modern technology at our disposal, new stars and solar systems are being discovered.

25 Which are the oldest types of observatories?

Long before the telescope was invented, even before the wheel, and when few people could write, men studied the sky.

They may have lived in wooden huts or dwellings built of sun-dried bricks – but they also built imposing and complex observatories.

Each morning, men greeted the sun with joy, stopping all work at sunset, when the moon appeared in the sky and it seemed to them that their Earth was being deserted. No wonder they wanted to look at the sky, trying to find the answers to their questions!

Between 3000 and 500 B.C. many observatories were built in China, Mesopotamia, Egypt, Phoenicia and India. In China in 2697 B.C., the first observation of an eclipse was recorded and in 2200 B.C. the first terraced pyramids were built in Mesopotamia.

Six hundred years before this, work had begun at Stonehenge in England on a huge observatory which took at least 1500 years to build.

26 Why is the Pole Star important?

The Pole Star is important because it is found exactly at the North Pole, or very near it, indicating north, and so helps us find our way.

It gets its name because of its position, at or near the North Celestial Pole. The Pole Star does not remain in the same position, moving because of what is known as the "precession of the equinoxes" when the Earth wobbles on its axis.

So, the position of the Pole or North Star has changed over the centuries.

Now, the Pole Star is Alpha Ursa Minor. Around 3000 B.C. it was the pole star of Alpha Draconic.

Looking into the future – towards 7500 A.D. it will be Alpha Cephei, and in 14000, Vega – until somewhere around the year 26000 A.D. the Pole Star will again be the star of our Alpha Ursa Minor (Polaris). Because this is so far away, it does not appear so bright to us. In fact, it is at least a thousand times brighter than our sun!

27 How is our Solar System made up?

The Solar System consists of all the planets, satellites, comets and other heavenly bodies which the sun maintains in orbit around itself.

There are nine planets in the Solar System, each of which, like Earth, rotates on its own axis as it travels around the sun.

Each rotation of the planet equals one day.

On Mercury, this is 1408 hours and on Venus almost 5832 hours.

On Earth, a day lasts 24 hours, on Mars 24 hours 30 minutes, on Jupiter less than 10 hours, Uranus 11, Neptune 16 and Pluto 153.

The galaxy of which the Solar System is part, is called the Milky Way with at least another 100,000,000,000 stars more than we can see.

Our galaxy is so vast that a ray of light travelling at 300,000 kilometres per second takes around 100,000 years to cross from one side to the other in terms of length, and "only" 20,000 years in terms of breadth.

28 What is the sun?

The sun is the Mother and Father of our Solar System, and none of us could exist without the sun! The sun is a star, but not one of the hottest. Its surface temperature is 6000° Centigrade – the hottest star is 50,000° Centigrade.

It is not one of the largest, being "only" 110 times bigger than Earth.

How does the sun produce such heat? The answer is quite simple.

Each second in the nucleus of the sun, 564,000,000 tons of hydrogen is melting, creating 560,000,000 tons of helium. The 4,000,000 tons "left over" in this huge melting process we call nuclear fusion is turned into energy radiating from the nucleus towards the surface.

The sun has been burning for 5,000,000,000 years. But the day will come when its hydrogen will be all used up, and the sun, like a car without petrol, will stop and "die".

When will this happen? In another 5,000,000,000 years...

29 How does an eclipse of the sun happen?

As the moon goes around the Earth, so the Earth goes around the sun. An eclipse happens when the moon comes between the Earth and the sun, which gradually disappears. How long it takes depends on the positions of the Earth, the sun and the moon, and the distance of the moon from the Earth. Total eclipses are visible only in some parts of the world, so although they are fairly frequent, one person may not see all of them.

30 How does an eclipse of the moon happen?

An eclipse of the sun happens when the moon comes between the Earth and the sun. An eclipse of the moon is when the Earth comes between the sun and the moon, when the moon is full.

When there is a new moon, the moon is between the sun and the earth, which is when an eclipse of the sun happens.

The numbers of eclipses which happen in a year vary from a minimum of two (in which case, they are both of the sun), to four (two of the sun and two of the moon – which is what happens most often), and a maximum of seven, which is five of the sun and two of the moon, or four of the sun and three of the moon. A total eclipse of the moon is not so impressive as a total eclipse of the sun!

There is nothing to fear from eclipses – but anyone who has watched the sun becoming obscured, and been plunged into sudden darkness at mid-morning can understand the panic of our ancestors.

31 Which travels faster – light or sound?

Nothing is faster than light. It travels at 300,000 kilometres a second. Sound is slower – "only" 330 metres a second! You can judge this difference in speed during a thunderstorm. Then, we see an electrical charge in lightning, and hear it in thunder. Count the seconds between seeing the lightning and hearing the thunder. Each second equals 330 metres! And when you count only two or three seconds, the storm is very near.

FLIGHT

Otto and the Stork

Otto and the Stork

SUNLIGHT STREAMED in through the window, warming the boys' heads as they listened to their teacher. The only other sound was the muffled voices of children, playing in the square below.

The schoolmaster's voice was quiet, too. But, he did not need to shout. One glance from him was enough to quell any disturbance – although there were some who longed to be out in the spring-time air, enjoying the sunshine.

Without warning, the master got up, continuing to speak. The boys held their breath. Slowly, the man walked between two rows of benches, then stopped in front of a seat beside a window, where a fair-haired boy, unaware of everything around him, looked out at the sky, fascinated.

In the silence of the class-room, the master's hand came down on the desk like a cannon. The boy jumped in his seat, turning around to look at the master, his blue eyes wide with fear.

The teacher looked furious, and the anxious faces of everyone in the class were turned towards him.

"Otto Lilienthal!" Still the man did not raise his voice. "Kindly tell your father that I wish to see him as soon as possible! You are wasting everyone's time at this school, so it is best that your parents take you away!"

Otto's father was not at all pleased when he heard what had happened.

"What were you looking at through the window during the Latin lesson?" he shouted.

"Th-the stork…" stammered Otto. He took a deep breath, trying to explain. "To see it fly interests me far more than learning Latin! The master was right! I learn nothing at this school! Instead, I want so much to learn other things. I want to understand how the stork can fly, how his wings work . . ."

Otto's father could see his son was serious. He decided to send Otto to a school where he could be happier.

And in a few months, his son was getting excellent marks and good reports from his tutors.

But during his spare time, he spoke of nothing but flight, studying the birds and reading all

he could about the flying machines which brave, daring inventors had built almost all over the world.

His passion, shared by his brother, Gustav, did not lessen with the years.

They built their own flying machine, and there was always a crowd of spectators in the Berlin neighbourhood who gathered to see the brothers hurling themselves into the air with their enormous, cloth wings.

"Man will be able to fly before long!" Otto told his brother. "We have not succeeded, because I have been doing things the wrong way! Storks are heavy birds, but their flight is slow and light. Their their wings are much lighter than the ones we make for ourselves...."

"I am sure," Otto continued, "that the secret lies in the shape of the wings, not their size. And we need an engine! Man does not have the muscle power to flap wings, but an engine could do that for us!"

"Yes, but there is no motor powerful enough nor light enough to be mounted on our machines!" Gustav pointed out.

"They are all too heavy! And, how many types of birds' wings have we studied? Yet, still you do not give up, Otto!"

That was true. Otto Lilienthal just could not give up trying.

And as years passed, the deeper his passion for flight became and the nearer a solution seemed. But so often, results were discouraging and the power of flight seemed as far away as ever.

"Somebody has to make sacrifices!" Otto murmured on 10th August 1896 to the doctor who attended him after yet another attempt – sadly, his last one.

So the eager, fair-haired boy, fascinated by the flight of the stork, did not overcome the problem of finding an engine.

But his studies and his experiments helped two young Americans, Orville and Wilbur Wright, who shared the same passion. And just seven years after the last flight of Otto Lilienthal, they felt themselves being lifted up off the ground, flying – just like the stork who had first inspired Otto!

1 Who was Icarus?

Greek legend tells how Minos, King of Crete, ordered a man called Daedalus to build a place to hold the Minotaur, his own monster son, half man, half bull. Daedalus built the labyrinth – a maze of tunnels. But Minos, fearing he might reveal the way out, imprisoned him and his son, Icarus. They escaped by making wings of wax and feathers. Ignoring his father's warnings, Icarus flew near the sun. The wax melted – and he fell into the sea.

2 How do birds fly?

Birds have a body "designed" for flight!

Their bones are light, with spaces full of air, body tapered. They have powerful muscles to move their wings, and a breastbone like a ship's prow to cut through the air! Their wings are specially shaped, (see 9 June), and, like the tail, have feathers of many shapes and textures, according to their job. Birds' flight can be "gliding" or "beating". In the gliding flight, the bird slides through the air, wings stretched out, quite still, carried by currents of air.

In "beating" flight, the bird moves its wings like oars, using its tail like a rudder to change direction.

Most birds take off almost vertically from land or water, body straight and wings beating quickly.

Once in the air, it leans its body forward and the wings beat more slowly.

For landing, the movements are reversed – straightening its body and beating its wings quickly before landing.

3 Are there birds which do not fly?

All birds have claws for walking and wings for flying. But many can only fly, or only walk, because they have under-developed wings or claws. Swifts, for example, have under-developed claws, but they are wonderful flyers. On the other hand, many of the larger birds have under-developed wings. Splendid ostriches and humble hens can only manage a few flaps – because they have a body which is too heavy for their wings.

4 Which birds are the strongest flyers?

When migrating, the Arctic Tern covers 17,000 kilometres! And even without migrating, swallows fly up to 1,000 kilometres a day. A Great Tit hen flies 100 kilometres back and forth to her nest to feed her young. As for speed, the Peregrine Falcon descends on its prey at 300 kilometres an hour – as fast as a Formula One racing car! A swallow can reach 200 kilometres an hour, the quail 90 kilometres and the shy turtledove around 70.

5 What problems did man face in flying?

Flying means lifting oneself off the ground and moving independently through the air.

A pebble thrown into the air will fly – but it is not independent, like birds who can lift themselves off the ground and move in the air at will.

When man first went into flight, he tried something lighter than air – balloons, filled first with hot air, later by gas. The balloon flew, but it was not easy to steer and had to be huge to carry passengers.

To take four people, the first airship had to be twice the length of a football pitch!

Trying to copy the birds, men built enormous wings which they moved with their arms and legs.

But nature did not give them strong enough muscles for this work and such experiments failed.

Otto Lilienthal set out the key factors in flight – that the secret of birds' wings was their shape, not size, and that man needed an engine. The aeroplane was born by putting those two things together.

6 What is the difference between hot air balloons and airships?

A balloon may be filled with hot air or gas, such as hydrogen or helium. In 1783, King Louis XVI saw a sheep, a duck, and a French hen become the first balloon passengers.

The balloon flies, or drifts, with the winds. It has to heat up or cool down, hot air allowing it to rise and descend.

The airship is a sort of torpedo-shaped balloon, but with steering mechanism and engines, so that it is not at the mercy of the wind.

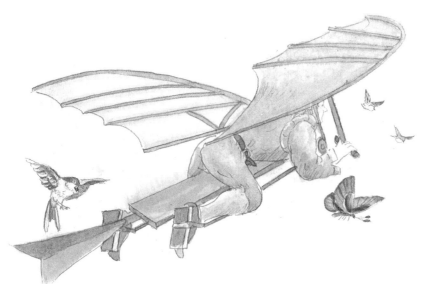

7 When were the first flying machines made?

Apart from balloons, a number of flying machines were invented, based on beating wings. Leonardo da Vinci, around 1500, was studying flight and designing machines, and many more men tried staying in the air by flapping wings after jumping from some high spot.

We may wonder at their courage and faith in the calculations they made – faith misplaced because beating wings proved useless in the end.

8 When was the first true air flight?

Man flew for the first time by a method heavier than air on 17th December 1903 at 10:35hrs.

The first man-made flight lasted only 12 seconds and covered just 40 metres. But soon after, three more were carried out, the last succeeding in covering 270 metres.

This historic event took place in Kittyhawk, North America, on the shores of the Atlantic Ocean.

There were five witnesses in all – as well as the two inventors, Orville and Wilbur Wright.

The aircraft built by the Wright brothers was based on the studies and experiments of Otto Lilienthal – a biplane without a front propeller, but with two rear propellers.

The wings were more than twelve metres long, and from the head to the tail of the aircraft, it measured 7.5 metres and 2.5 metres high, with a benzine engine of twelve-horse power which powered the two propellers.

The aircraft had wheels, and for landing, it had to run on a wooden rail, controlled by means of a joystick to turn the wings.

And so, the Wright brothers, bicycle manufacturers by trade, saw the results of their long, careful studies as well as experiments made by other pioneers in flight.

Their aircraft was called The Flyer. This fragile biplane made of wood and cloth succeeded because its inventors had found a way of applying the skill of the birds which Leonardo da Vinci had first studied.

9 How does an aeroplane fly?

To fly, an aeroplane needs thrust and lift. Thrust comes from the propellers thrusting through the air, making the aeroplane move forward. Lift comes from the air and wing shape – flat underneath, rounded on top.

Air flows faster above the wing, because it has further to go. This makes the air pressure above lower than the pressure beneath it. The higher pressure below pushes up against the wing and produces lift.

10 What is a VTOL aircraft?

VTOL stands for Vertical Take Off and Landing.

It applies to aircraft which, thanks to jet engines, can ascend and descend vertically.

However, "vertically" does not mean with the nose of the aircraft pointing upwards and then straightening out, once it is in the air.

Instead, the aircraft lifts off immediately into the air without needing a runway to take off and land.

Once in the air, the engines accelerate up as usual and the VTOL behaves the same as other aircraft.

One variation of the VTOL is the STOL – Short Take Off and Landing.

This type of aircraft only needs a little more space to land and take off, than is required by the VTOL.

With care, STOL aircraft can land and take off within a maximum of 200 metres.

Then, as with the VTOL aircraft, once in the air, they are just the same as other aircraft.

11 What is a variable wing-span aircraft?

Aircraft do not beat their wings like birds – but some can open and close them. This type of "Swing-Wing" aircraft has variable wing span, designed to help the aircraft at both low and high speeds.

The picture shows the various phases of opening and closing the wings during the different moments in flight – the take-off with the wings open, then less and less, until, at the speed required, the wings are closed.

12 Who are Air Traffic Controllers?

Air Traffic Controllers are technical specialists who operate in the Control Centre of an airport. The Centre is also called the Control Tower, because the building is the highest in the airport. The reason for this is because the radar scanner on top has to range over the airport in all directions without obstacles.

The radar picks up signals from aerials and transmitters and shows them on the Controllers' screens.

When they see on their screens that an aircraft is coming in to land, the Controllers radio the pilot to tell him the route to follow in the sky and the runway on which to land. They also indicate where an aircraft should take off.

Controllers have a demanding and difficult job, not only because of the increasing amount of air traffic. They also have to take into account things such as wind forces at different heights and the risk of fog, before being able to give directions to the pilot.

13 What is the Sound Barrier?

Nowadays, aircraft can fly at astonishing speeds.

None have yet gone faster than light – but quite a few have gone faster than sound!

Sound – as we have seen in the Question and Answer for 31st May, is a "snail" compared to light. Still, it travels at 330 metres a second, equivalent to around 1200 kilometres an hour!

Aircraft which travel faster than the speed of sound are called "supersonic".

Their presence in the sky does not go unnoticed! Everyone knows they are there because of a deafening BANG!

But, why this noise?

The supersonic BANG is caused by the fact that when an aircraft flies at a speed near to that of sound, the air puts up a strong resistance, creating in front of the aircraft a barrier, which we call the Sound Barrier.

Of course, it is not a "barrier" to the aircraft because it flies through easily. But it is this break-through which produces the deafening BANG.

14 When did Air Mail begin?

The first air mail delivery we know of was the olive branch which the dove brought back to Noah to tell him that the flood was over!

But as a regular service whereby correspondence and parcels could be carried by aeroplane, Air Mail began in Italy.

On the 20th May 1917, during the First World War, an air mail service began from Turin to Rome and vice versa.

It was the First World War which brought to people's attention the many advantages of using aircraft, with all countries eager to use this new method of transport and attack.

After that there was a race to improve and develop aircraft, to make them more and more fast, safe and efficient, to build aerodromes and install safety equipment.

Soon aircraft proved to be just as important in peace-time, in providing transport for long-distance travellers, carrying cargo and giving an air mail service.

15 When was pigeon post first used?

The habit of pigeons to "fly back home" was noted by the Ancient Babylonians. The Phoenicians, too, never left for their adventurous journeys without a good supply of pigeons to take news back home.

And Ancient Egyptians built a network of pigeon towers watched over by special caretakers. These were the official "posts" to which the pigeons flew back, papyrus messages tied to their legs.

Romans even enlisted pigeons in the army!

Each Roman Legion had pigeon-carriers with five or six thousand birds. Thanks to them, those in Rome got news from all over the Roman Empire!

In 1870, the besieged city of Paris communicated with the rest of France by pigeon post, with the birds carrying over a million dispatches. The Parisians erected a monument in Neuilly Park to Eolo, the most famous, who flew eleven times from Paris to Tours.

More recently, pigeons carried important messages during the Second World War.

16 Who made the first flight across the Atlantic?

At 7.52am on 20th May 1927, Charles Lindbergh took off on board his aircraft, *The Spirit of St. Louis*, to fly from New York to Paris without stopping.

Pessimists thought there was only a very slim chance he would succeed. To keep alive, he had only five rolls, five tins of meat and two flasks of water. He had kept cargo to a minimum, in order to carry the maximum amount of fuel. There was no room for a parachute or radio!

People were so impressed by his courage, they watched his aircraft through binoculars.

But when he was crossing the Atlantic Ocean there was nobody to see anything, apart from a few fishermen.

Aircraft at this time did not have a closed cockpit or air conditioning. So, when he was caught in a storm, Lindbergh's map got very wet. When it was foggy, he only had his experience as a pilot to save himself from getting lost – and the aircraft's fragile wings became coated with ice in the cold air of the Atlantic.

But after 23 hours non-stop flying, Lindbergh came in sight of England! He could see fishermen, ships, people looking up at him through binoculars and waving!

And at ten o'clock that evening, he saw the lights of Paris, the runway lit up in his honour and crowds waiting to welcome him in triumph. But, after flying for 33 hours and covering almost 5800 kilometres, he longed for a nice, soft bed before any celebrations!

17 How does a glider fly?

A glider is an aircraft without an engine which makes use of the natural currents of air.

Gliders can be catapulted into the air (soaring or sailing), then flying solo in descent (hovering).

An aircraft may also tow a glider to the place where it will land. Once the landing place is in sight, the glider pilot will unhook the tow-rope or cable so that he can land the glider in free flight.

18 How does a hang-glider fly?

With a hang-glider, a person can fly by gliding along on currents of air.

A strong, synthetic covering is fastened to the aluminium framework of its triangular wings. And wearing a harness, the pilot lays across a horizontal section between the wings and controls the flight by means of a trapeze bar which alters the shape of the wings and so catches the air currents at different angles. Micro-lights are motorised hang gliders.

19 When was the parachute invented?

The parachute is a device designed to reduce the speed of a fall.

The first person to think of the idea was Leonardo da Vinci. His design was rather like a pyramid with a square-shaped base.

The first parachute descent was by Andre-Jacques Garnerin in 1797. He jumped from a balloon, using a parachute of his own design. His brother perfected it and his daughter, Elisa, toured Europe and America doing parachute jumps for exhibitions.

Despite the fact that they were known to save lives, parachutes were used only towards the end of the First World War in military aircraft.

The actual parachute is a circle of 50 square metres, made of very strong silk or nylon which has to be very light, weighing only 5 – 6 kilogrammes for all those square metres. From the circle hangs a thick circle of ropes on which is hooked the body (human or an object). These ropes are also made of silk or nylon, strong but light.

20 Who invented the helicopter?

Leonardo da Vinci had the idea of a helicopter. But the first working model using a small steam engine was built by Enrico Forlanini in 1877 – almost 30 years before the Wright brothers. The helicopter flies thanks to a rotor made up of rotor-blades. Speed is varied by the rotor and inclination, leaning one way or the other. It can fly in all directions, hover, lift off and descend vertically, with the tail propeller giving stability.

21 How can people fly in space?

The science which studies methods of flight into space is called astronautics.

From ancient times, man has dreamed of being able to travel towards other heavenly bodies – but they had to wait for Isaac Newton to establish the laws of motion which would help make this possible. And after Newton, it took another two hundred years to achieve rocket propulsion.

Finally, in 1957, Russia launched into orbit Sputnik, the first artificial satellite.

There were many problems to overcome. Sputnik needed to have speeds of 8 – 11 kilometres a second. The second problem was the return to Earth – needing to know exactly where Earth would be on its axis at the moment when the space-craft landed, after weeks, months or years from the launch. The engines, materials to be used, methods of communicating with Earth... every single detail had to be studied thoroughly before the launch into space.

22 What is the Space Shuttle?

The Space Shuttle is really a space bus!

It was developed in the United States to take a crew of eight plus their materials into space, then return to Earth, to be used for other space journeys.

The Space Shuttle is launched into a pre-arranged orbit by two rockets, each supplied with a parachute. When they have done their work, they glide to Earth, where they are recovered.

Then, once the astronauts have finished their mission, the Space Shuttle returns to the orbit of the Earth. Having wings, it glides down, assisted by a parachute at the rear to slow down the speed.

The Space Shuttle is very young, dating only from 1981. If in the future direct journeys can be made to some space base, it will be the Space Shuttle which will take passengers, equipment and so on.

And, who knows? The day may come when there is a Space Shuttle service for people working in space for a few years – or even those taking short holidays...

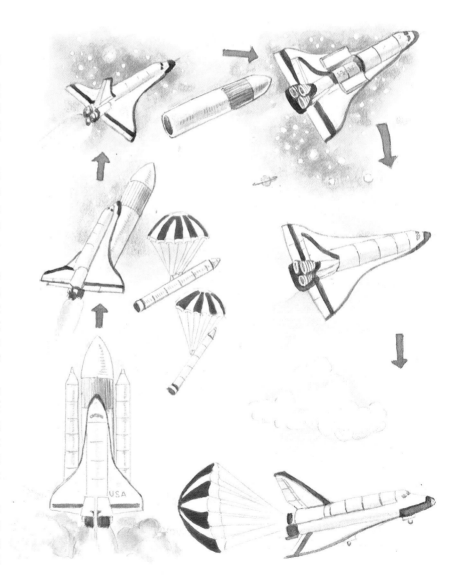

23 Is it easy to fly a kite?

The kite uses currents of air, flying rather like a glider being towed. If you want to make it fly, you need a day when there is a lot of movement in the air.

Nowadays, kites come in all different shapes including amazing birds and creatures such as dragons, with long fluttering tails. They can be made to perform complex acrobatic movements, swooping low to the ground and high up in the air. There is quite an art to flying a kite!

As well as being a toy, more complex types of kite have been used in weather observation.

The American scientist Benjamin Franklin used a kite in some of his experiments, which gave him valuable help when it came to inventing the lightning conductor.

Franklin was convinced that lightning was due to electrical charges. Knowing that these electrical charges were attracted to pointed objects, he thought of a way to make the lightning follow a safe course, so that the electricity could be released safely into the ground, instead of striking trees, spires roofs or bell towers and causing damage.

So Franklin made a kite with a metal point, which he flew during a fierce storm.

And, as he expected, the metal point attracted the lightning, which struck it.

Franklin had risked his life – but he knew now that his idea worked.

Lightning conductors soon began appearing – metal rods fixed to the walls of buildings which attracted the lightning and took the electricity down into the ground without any danger or damage.

24 How does a bat fly?

Bats fly by using echoes of sound-waves, like echo-sounders on ships. As it flies, the bat's movements give out waves of ultrasound (sounds of higher frequency than those heard by the human ear).

These bounce off the surroundings, returning like an echo. These echoes tell the bat the shape, size and distance of an object or animal so accurately that a bat can fly safely between the branches of a tree.

25 What is a U.F.O.?

The initials U.F.O. stand for Unidentified Flying Object.

These objects can appear in the sky or on a radar screen as something we do not quite understand. Usually they appear to travel at great speed and then vanish without trace.

Often, we find that a sighting of a U.F.O. can be traced to something like a mirage, or a trick of the light from things such as weather balloons and so on.

But many U.F.O. sightings seem to defy explanation, making many people curious enough to go "sky-watching", hoping to see a U.F.O. of their own.

Many believe, too, that Earth is not the only planet in the Universe with human life.

So, perhaps the U.F.O. is a space-ship carrying people from other planets, just as curious and as eager as we are to watch, to discover and to communicate.

Until Science can give us the facts, all we have are stories about the beings we call "E.T." those "Extra Terrestrials" visiting Earth on their flying saucer – otherwise known as a U.F.O.

26 Are there any plants which fly?

There are plants which can fly and move in the air.

These are the ones which can reproduce due to their seeds and pollen being carried on the wind.

To make the task of the wind easier and to ensure that as many new plants as possible will grow, nature has given lots of help when it comes to flying!

For example, pollen is made up of very small grains, each with tiny little sacs of air to help it fly further.

Pollen is the male reproduction cell

To father a new plant, it has to come in contact with feminine cells, which it is more likely to meet some distance from its mother plant.

Some plants have seed pods which, when dry, „shoot" their seeds away from them.

Trees such as elm, sycamore and maple produce fruit which have little propellers.

So, with their propellers, these fruits can be carried on the wind, away from the mother plant, where it can find plenty of space to grow.

27 Are there fish which can fly?

Yes – some fish have very supple pectoral fins very similar to birds' wings.

These are the Flying Fish and they leap up to two metres out of the water, covering up to thirty metres in free flight gliding.

The speed they reach is a remarkable 50 kilometres an hour!

Flying Fish or "Sea Swallows" live in tropical seas, but other types are also found in the southern Mediterranean.

28 How does flight help man?

Almost from the time they were invented, aeroplanes have carried passengers and goods.

They also transport soldiers and weapons in war-time, and their use has now become so widespread that they regularly carry out important social services.

Many hospitals in big cities throughout the world can call helicopters to take medical staff quickly to the scene of an accident, then ferry the injured back to hospital.

Very often, helicopters are also used for carrying seriously ill patients and delivering medicines to emergency situations in the shortest possible time.

Police Forces can use helicopters to survey streets and report on traffic problems for the benefit of motorists.

Fire-watchers and forest rangers have at their disposal giant flying tankers which can carry many litres of sea water to put out fires, doing this far more quickly and effectively than if they were on earth.

By patrolling in light aircraft or helicopters, the forest rangers and fire-watchers can also quickly see the faintest column of smoke which signals the beginning of a fire. They can then alert the emergency services by radio for fast action.

In the case of natural disasters, such as floods and earthquakes, helicopters can carry people to safety.

And both aeroplanes and helicopters can drop food, clothes, tents and medicines by parachute at camps and field hospitals.

29 Who are the flying doctors?

There are some countries in the world with vast, desolate areas which would prevent any doctor reaching a patient in need of urgent medical help.

In Kenya, for example, a person could be near to death because of a snake bite whilst crossing the Kenya National Park. The distance is so vast that the victim would probably not be alive by the time they reached hospital.

And so the Flying Doctor service came into being.

The service is called by radio – a person just calls, says what has happened and where the patient is and the doctor flies in as soon as possible.

Countries such as Australia and Canada make widespread use of the Flying Doctor Services to provide medical cover to those remote areas where conventional surface transport might take many more hours or even days. Although fixed wing aeroplanes are faster, helicopters, may be used because of their ability to land in very confined spaces like forest clearings or hospital roofs.

30 What is aerial archaeology?

Charles Lindbergh, the courageous pilot who was the first to cross the Atlantic non-stop, had another passion – aerial archaeology.

Staff employed by museums and universities have flown over the forests of Central America. Keeping at a fairly low height, they have discovered the remains of towns built by the Incas and the Aztecs.

Tracing archaeological remains by any other means is completely unthinkable in such areas – people would have no means of knowing exactly where to go in order to organise an expedition on foot.

But, from the air, people can quickly see so much of the Earth. Aerial photographs of fields and vegetation reveal old villages – because the ground above an old construction appears clearer and greener, marking out buildings, streets, ancient camps and underground rivers, giving archaeologists a complete picture of a whole site which would otherwise take years of work.

TRAVEL

Going on Holiday

Going on Holiday

JOHN HOPED HIS DAD was going the right way.

Towing a caravan along a narrow, winding road without a single house in sight meant he had to drive very slowly and the car seemed to be showing signs of breaking down.

An hour had passed since they'd heard on the car radio about tailbacks on all motorways and that drivers were advised to find other routes.

At first, everything was all right. But gradually, houses and buildings became fewer and fewer, before disappearing altogether. Now, there was just open countryside.

John was glad when Dad stopped the car at last.

"We seem to be right in the mountains!" Dad burst out irritably, looking all around. "Miles from the sea!"

"Look over there!" cried Grandpa suddenly. He was pointing to what seemed to be a mountain hut with a few animal pens, farm buildings and a bit of grazing land.

"Might as well walk over," sighed Dad, "if only to stretch our legs!"

The cool breeze was very refreshing and they all felt a lot happier when a boy told them that they were only about half an hour's drive away from their holiday destination.

"That's a relief!" Dad grinned. "Come on, everyone let's be on our way!"

"What's the hurry?" said Grandpa. "Let's stay here and rest awhile!"

Soon, the boy had filled a stone jar with clear, running water from an outdoor tap, and they all stretched themselves out under a big, leafy tree enjoying a picnic.

They began talking and the boy told them his name was James.

He was 18 years old, he said, and studying to be a vet. He lived in a village nearby and in the summer months, he took it in turns with his brothers to bring their goats to pasture.

As James went on talking, John began looking around at the trees, the goats and sheep wandering here and there, the cows and the wooden hut...

Then, something nudged his shoulder, making him turn round sharply.

It was a white goat with a little, white beard!

Laughing, John sprung to his feet – and when he broke off a

piece of his roll, the goat licked every last crumb from his hand! Soon, the goat had eaten a whole roll – and John was his friend!

"Don't go too far!" called Dad, as the goat followed John towards a cluster of trees.

"Oh, don't worry!" said Grandpa, getting to his feet.

He picked up a stick and strolled away, whistling, leaving John's mum and dad dozing under the tree.

It was John who woke them up, the little white goat trotting behind!

"There's trout in that stream!" he cried. "Grandpa's going to make me a fishing rod!"

It seemed to be no time at all before James appeared again, this time with some milk and honey, ready for afternoon tea.

John and his family had hardly begun, when there was a strange bleating noise.

"There's something wrong with that goat!" cried James, jumping up and running towards the hut.

"Can I go and help him?" asked John. His mother nodded.

"We'll go together!" she said.

At the hut, she made some of her special herb tea, ready for James to give to the little goat to drink. John wanted to help – but he soon found that the job was not as easy as it looked! He was trying so hard, he did not even see the door opening.

"Time to go, John!" Dad said.

"But I can't go!" cried John. "The little goat is ill!"

"You have done enough," said his mother. "Come along, now."

They turned away. But when John saw the caravan, he burst out, "Grandpa said we could go fishing tomorrow, then cook some trout - - -"

"John," Dad sighed, "it's not like the seaside here! There are no ice-cream parlours, pizza bars, not even television - - -"

"Well," Grandpa put in, "I know I'd rather stay here. You can pick me up on the way home!"

"Can I stay, too?" asked John.

Mum and Dad looked at each other. "We'll have to do some shopping before we make that fishing rod, John!" smiled Dad. "I'll enjoy reading those books I bought some months ago! But, what will you do without television - - -?"

And before John could say anything, the little goat's bleating answered Dad's question.

1 How did people travel in prehistoric times?

Even before men began putting wheels on vehicles around six thousand years ago, people were travelling. Horses, dromedaries, camels and llamas carried goods and people, and were absolutely necessary in mountains and desert zones.

In the far north, skis and sledges pulled by dogs, horses and reindeer helped people to travel over the snow – quite apart from boats in which people could travel on water.

2 Which were the main waterways?

Men soon discovered that rivers were "roads" – ideal for travel and almost as easy as overland. If they did not want to follow the current, they could turn their boats around by being towed or pulled from the bank.

But some rivers were too rough for boats. Others had treacherous river beds or were dangerous because of drought or flooding.

In Africa, men used the Congo, and parts of the Nile, but in Asia only the tributary rivers were suitable.

In North America, men travelled the area of the Great Lakes and the Mississippi-Missouri, and the Amazon in South America.

Europeans could travel most easily because nearly all rivers were close by and many flowed into each other.

For example, from the Baltic Sea, along the Dvina and the Dnieper, honey, ceramics, animal hides and timbers were brought to Constantinople – now the Turkish capital of Istanbul – heart of the Byzantine Empire.

Further east, the Volga flowed to the Caspian Sea, or the River Don then on to the Black Sea.

From Denmark, men journeyed south following the Elba, and to the heart of Europe, going along the Rhine from the North Sea.

The Loire crosses France, flowing on to the Atlantic, whilst the Rhone flows into the Mediterranean. The Po River links the Adriatic Sea with the Western Alps, and the Adige links up with Central Europe.

Countless smaller rivers also brought goods, men – and ideas.

3 What were the main European routes?

North Africa, the Middle East, Byzantium (now Turkey), Southern Italy, Spain and Southern France were linked by a busy river trade. Merchants and sailors from Crete, Phoenecia and then Greece met at special ports which became busy markets, where they could exchange their own goods with Eastern produce. If the market was at the mouth of a river, goods could come from miles inland, brought from boat to boat, river to river.

4 Where were the first roads built?

Although the wheel and travel by wheeled vehicles began 6000 years ago, men were covering great distances before that on foot and horseback – but most of all, along the rivers. But because there were no roads, wheeled vehicles were used mainly for exercise or for going only short distances.

This is why the great ancient civilisations developed either along rivers or the coast.

There were the Ancient Egyptians on the Nile, the Mesopotamians along the rivers Tigris and Euphrates and the Cretes, Phoenecians and Greeks along the coast – all of which reduced the problem of communication between different countries.

But when the Persian Empire established itself in the Middle East and found there were rivers in only a part of Mesopotamia, the communication problem became urgent.

So, the Persians linked together the twenty provinces which comprised their Empire with a road network, branching off the Royal Road which went from what is now Iran to Sardi, in Turkey. Messengers rode on horseback along the Royal Road, bringing news to their sovereign and the empire.

This road network covered 3000 kilometres, with postal stations and inns along the way where riders could also change horses.

Everyone from merchants to peasants used this service, and when America instituted a similar one more than 2000 years later, they called it the *Pony Express*.

5 How were the Roman roads built?

The Ancient Romans were masters at building roads. On a bed of sand and gravel they put a layer of crushed stone and lime, then a layer of gravel and lime, and finally the paving stones, rounded to allow water to drain away. Wherever Roman roads were built, so they enriched lives, not only in trade but also in enabling people to travel and exchange customs and ideas – leading to the closer unity of a vast empire.

6 How did the Ancient Romans travel?

On their beautiful roads, the Romans first began travelling on foot.

For moving around in towns or when living in the country, lords and ladies travelled on litters, carried on the shoulders of their slaves.

Mules and horses were the most common methods of travel, but there were a variety of wheeled vehicles, too.

To go on long journeys, there was a two-wheeled chariot which the Romans called an *essedum*, strong and able to move quickly, plus the *cisium*, which was lighter and faster.

The *carruca dormitoria* had four wheels. It was comfortable, richly decorated and with enough room for passengers to sleep. This was the most luxurious method of travel in Ancient Roman times. Other vehicles included the *carrus*, a wagon with four spoked wheels, and the *plaustram*, pulled by oxen and with high wheels, mostly used by countrymen to take their products into the towns.

7 What were the Mayan roads like?

The Mayan Empire extended through jungles, swamps, mountains and plains. To link cities with each other as well as the coast, the Mayans built roads, many of which were almost 100 kilometres long. These were built on a base of limestone with a tightly compressed layer of damp gravel. The Spanish who used them afterwards found them ideal, up to 4.5 metres wide, and perfectly flat, 1.20 metres above ground level.

8 What sort of roads did the Incas build?

The Incas, like the Romans, knew that roads were necessary for the movement of armies, to keep all parts of the empire in touch with each other and to increase trade.

The Inca Empire had a network of roads, all leading into two main roads – the Royal Road along the Andes from the northern border of Rio Ancasmayo, across Ecuador, Peru, Bolivia, Argentina and ending at Chile – and the coastal road from Tumbes, crossing Peru and Chile then joining the Royal Road.

The Royal Road was over 5000 kilometres long, the coastal road over 4000 kilometres.

Smaller roads led into the Andes valleys, strong suspension bridges going across rocks in jungles and over mountains at breath-taking heights – the highest was at 5150 metres! They were usually just over 7 metres wide, including two low walls at either side.

The Incas did not know the wheel and there were no horses in South America in ancient times.

Llamas carried goods, not people.

So, the Incas travelled on foot, except for important people who were carried on litters.

Royal messengers had the right of way. Young sprinters able to run 2.5 kilometres in ten minutes were stationed at special places ready to leave by day or night, one runner passing a message to the next.

With this relay system, they needed only five days and nights for a message to get from Quito to Cuzco, the Inca capital, 2000 kilometres away.

9 Do people still use waterways for transport?

At the end of the 19th century, the Industrial Revolution in England brought an enormous increase in goods being made – goods which had to be sold and therefore transported.

But there were few roads at this time and the pace was very slow – so many canals were built.

And although the railways took away a great deal of canal traffic, both rivers and canals are still used for transport today.

10 Who designed the canal at Corinth?

Before the canal at Corinth, ships had to sail all around the Greek coast to get from Italy or Spain to Athens. Cutting through this narrow neck of land was the idea of Julius Caesar, but Nero started it, only managing to cut 1.7 kilometres of the 6.3 kilometres necessary.

After Nero, almost 2000 years passed, until, in 1881, work resumed and in 1893, the canal at Corinth was opened to shipping.

11 When was the train invented?

The first railway line in 1825 went the 34 kilometres from Stockton to Darlington in the north of England. The train was pulled by a steam locomotive built by George Stephenson.

Five years after came the first passenger train, also pulled by a locomotive designed by Stephenson.

Reaching a speed of 20 kilometres an hour, a remarkable achievement for the time, it served Liverpool and Manchester.

The regularity and speed of the service, together with fares on a level with those of a stagecoach ensured that railways were soon a success.

Once the railways were established and locomotives became more efficient, designers began to pay attention to the comfort of passengers.

Instead of open trucks with planks of wood for seats, carriages became more comfortable and elegant, even luxurious, spreading the habit of rail travel to all types of people.

12 What is The Orient Express?

The Orient Express is not a train, but a route – a direct railway line linking London and Paris with the south east capitals of Europe – Bucharest, Istanbul and Athens.

Beginning in the 1880's, the trains on this line are sitting rooms on wheels, tastefully furnished and with meals served to the highest standard. A person can meet princes, writers, business tycoons .... all travelling out of necessity or for enjoyment.

July

13 What were the first major railway tunnels?

With the advent of the railways, to overcome sloping heights and sharp curves, tunnels had to be built through mountains. In Europe, the biggest challenge was the Alps, where tunnelling was a true feat of engineering.

The Frejus tunnel between France and Italy which took 15 years to build (1857 – 1871) is 16.5 kilometres long and the Simplon, which took almost 9 years, from 1898 to 1906, is almost 20 kilometres long.

14 What is a narrow gauge railway?

On a railway, the rails are a certain distance apart, and this is called the gauge.

The rails for the first-ever railway, between Stockton and Darlington in 1825, were 56.5" – 1.435 metre.

This measurement is the usual or "standard gauge" used for railways in Europe, North America, China and on recently-built railways in Japan.

There are also some wider track gauges – almost 1.70 metre in Spain and Portugal, Argentina, India and Russia.

So, narrow gauge railways are those where the distance between the rails is narrower, usually 39" or 1 metre.

These are used in South Africa, Japan, Thailand, Indonesia, Brazil, Africa, South America and on numerous other smaller railways in almost every part of the world.

Trains made for narrow gauge railways cannot run anywhere else, because their wheels, too, have to be a certain distance apart.

15 What is an Underground System?

In 1863, the Metropolitan Underground Railway opened in London, linking up the mainline railway stations above.

The advantages were that the Underground did not jam the streets with traffic, and people could travel across the city far quicker than in any other form of transport.

After London, Budapest had the next underground system in 1896, then Paris (1900), Berlin (1902) and New York (1904).

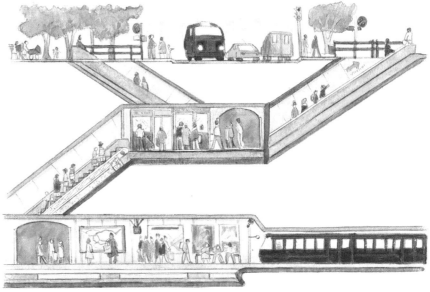

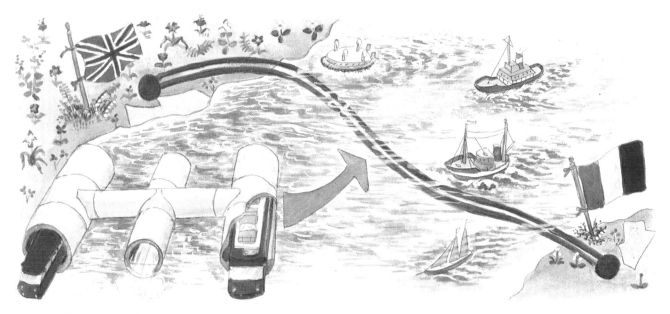

16 How was the Channel Tunnel built?

On 22nd September 1990, the wall between the English and French-built sections of the Channel Tunnel was broken through.

One newspaper reported this with the headline "GREAT BRITAIN CEASES TO BE AN ISLAND FOR THE FIRST TIME SINCE THE ICE AGE!"

In fact, when ice covered the whole of northern Europe, it was possible to reach England by foot. Only with the melting of the covering of ice, about 8000 years ago, did Great Britain become an island.

With the Channel Tunnel, people will be able to make an overland crossing once more, this time by car and train.

It took three years working 40 metres below the sea bed, before the English/French meeting and the tunnel is expected to be in use between Folkestone and Calais some time in 1994.

The Channel Tunnel consists of three tunnels – a central tunnel for cars, coaches and other road transport, and a tunnel either side for trains going in opposite directions.

Over twelve thousand men have been employed so far and at either terminus, a station will be built.

These "tunnel tigers" work hard. Each morning the French workers look at a special chart to see the progress made the previous day.

On 20th September 1990, the workers actually saw the first result – a 5cms hole breaking the last barrier, and "feeling the air coming through from the other half".

17 When was the car invented?

Attempts to build a vehicle which could move by means of an engine go back some time – even Leonardo da Vinci thought about it. The main problem was the engine.

Then in 1877, the Austrian Siegfried Marcus built a 4-stroke engine which, three years later, Daimler adapted for a car.

Daimler continued to experiment, until he got the right engine – light, fast, easy to use and able to be put on a wheeled carriage.

18 What were the "Devil's Bridges"?

Bridges, both large and small, were rare in ancient times. And when people saw these structures crossing wide rivers, many were sure that men could not have built them by skill and hard work – the devil must have done it!

In the Middle Ages, many bridges were thought to be the work of the devil, but bridges were objects of fear long before that.

When Julius Caesar wanted to impress the Germans who were trying to invade Gaul, he built a wooden bridge across the Rhone, crossed over, and then destroyed it.

The Germans decided that somebody who could do such a thing was not to be underestimated and stayed firmly on their side of the river!

Today, notable bridges include Austria's Europa Bridge,190 metres high; the Golden Gates Bridge, California, supported by steel girders 93cms thick, and the bridge over Lake Ponchartrain on the Mississippi delta, over 48 kilometres long.

19 Is motor racing only for people to watch?

Men and animals will always rise to a challenge.

Even a game of tennis between friends is a competition to test the physical condition of the players, the state of the field of play, the efficiency of rackets and shoes, the effectiveness of a tactic or training.

But with something like a Formula One rally, it is not always easy to see that the race is only the outward show for months of hard work.

Racing car teams test the latest methods before they are built into ordinary cars to help millions of motorists – brakes, suspension, lights and tyres – which have shown their worth and proved their efficiency in the extremely harsh and challenging conditions of the race track.

The first car rally in history was the Paris to Rouen in 1894.

Of one hundred and two competitors, only fourteen crossed the finishing line, led by a man called De Dion in a steam-driven car with an average speed of 24 kilometres an hour.

20 How did ancient civilisations discover the wheel?

With wheelbarrows and pulley wheels, men found they could carry, then lift stone for building.

But how did ancient civilisations build pyramids and temples without the help of a wheel?

They shifted the stones by means of manpower – or they rolled loaded sledges across round logs which they then laid again in front of the sledge until they reached the chosen position or a sloping piece of ground.

21 How does the electric car work?

The electric car is like any other battery-powered object, from a toy to a razor. But, what sort of batteries does a car need to make it work? And how much driving time does it give before it needs to be re-charged?

These are the problems waiting to be solved.

Whilst use of electric cars would decrease pollution, helping to make the sky blue in many industrial areas, they would be costly, small, needing cumbersome batteries, unable to go far and not very fast, either.

Yet despite all this, the development of an electric car is still a worthy cause. So perhaps we shall see them on the road before too long.

Perhaps at this moment there is a student who instead of listening to a teacher, is looking out of the window – not at storks, like the aviator Otto Lilienthal, but at children playing with battery-powered toys, working out what we need to make an electric car become a reality.

22 When was the bicycle invented?

Although bicycles without pedals or means of steering appeared in the early 1800's, the fore-runner of the modern pedal-driven bicycle was the "velocipede" built in France by Michaux in 1865. Over the years it was improved, especially with air-filled tyres to make cycling more comfortable.

By 1890, the bicycle was much the same as it is now. Now, over 100 years afterwards, more people are using them to get around town.

23 What is a cycle lane?

In modern cities, the amount of traffic often makes it difficult, if not dangerous, to travel on a bicycle.

Therefore, because so many people have gone back to using a bicycle, especially around city areas, a number of authorities have provided a special lane, to one side of a roadway.

This is the cycle lane, or cycle track, on which cars are forbidden. Not even parking for a while is allowed unless drivers want to face a fine or some angry cyclists!

More and more of these cycle lanes are appearing all over the world, together with special bicycle parks – like car parks – with fixed stands and padlocked chains to avoid theft. Many of these bicycle parks have been built under shelter to protect the machines from rain.

With the constant increase in the number of cyclists, many authorities see cycle lanes and bicycle parks as a way of helping to reducing traffic problems and easing congestion around our large towns.

24 What is a mountain bike?

As the name says – the mountain bike is a bicycle adapted for riding on mountains.

To make it easier for the cyclist to climb steep slopes, it is equipped with a minimum of three extra cogs or gears on the front chain ring and six extra cogs on the back wheel, giving a maximum of four cogs on the front chain ring and seven cogs on the back wheel. With four front and seven rear cogs, the cyclist can obtain up to twenty-eight gear changes – the more cogs, the more gears there are, making it possible to go up an incline of 45 degrees – if the legs are up to it!

The mountain bike is also light and strong, enabling the cyclist to rise and descend at high speed, and supporting the body over holes, stones and the roots of trees.

So, you won't get the best out of a mountain bike by riding it only in city areas. Instead, it should be used to go with friends into the woods or country areas, discovering places far from busy streets.

25 What sort of wagons did the American pioneers travel in?

The pioneers who crossed the plains of America were brave and hardworking. They suffered such harsh conditions on their journeys to find a land which offered them a future.

Horses pulled the heavy four-wheeled wagons which were covered by cloth pulled tight over a circular wooden framework which protected both goods and people, the wagons moving in a long line.

There were many risks in making the journey, not only the dangers of the trail, crossing rivers and going over high mountains, but also hostile Red Indians and bandits, horses going lame, illnesses and wagons breaking.

Most of the pioneers were farm-workers. At the end of their long journey, they expected to find a fertile, flat land where they could build houses and be able to make a living. So the wagons held not only things for the journey, but also farming equipment seeds, pots and plates – everything needed for them to begin a new life.

26 How do people travel across snow?

Wearing ordinary shoes, people would slip on snow and ice.

Instead, they need snow-shoes, similar to tennis rackets to look at, with a cord mesh threaded into a wooden frame. These are tied to shoes, and they prevent slipping by distributing the weight of a person over a surface which is bigger than their feet. Skis and sleighs work in the same way. Snow-shoes, skis and sleighs have been used since ancient times.

Today, there are also motor vehicles with special pneumatic tyres which use spikes or chains rather than treads so that they can grip the snow, just as bears and snow leopards use their claws to gain extra traction.

Four wheel drive vehicles are another effective way of increasing traction in snowy regions, especially where they are able to divert power from any slipping wheels to those wheels with better grip.

Probably the most successful form of transport in the worst snow conditions uses caterpillar tracks rather than wheels.

27 How can dogs help in an avalanche?

Rescue organisations use specially trained dogs to help rescue people in mountain areas. Most famous are Saint Bernard dogs, so called because they were bred by monks at the home of Saint Bernard. These large dogs with their thick coats are able to follow tracks through snow drifts and track down people trapped by an avalanche. Once, the monks put little flasks of brandy on their collars to warm the victims as they awaited help.

28 What journey did Lewis and Clark make?

In 1803, Napoleon decided to sell Louisiana in North America. At that time it covered an area of more than 2,000,000,000 square kilometres. Thomas Jefferson, the United States President, bought it for $15,000,000,000, thus doubling the territory of the U.S.A.

Inhabited by Indians and a few French settlers, Louisiana was largely unexplored. So, President Jefferson organised an expedition so that more could be known.

He gave the command to Captain Meriwether Lewis, who chose as his companion Captain William Clark.

Their aim was to set down the route of the Missouri River, crossing the Rocky Mountains to the Pacific Ocean, going from east to west, collecting information and making peace with the Indians as they went.

This amazing expedition began on 14th March 1804 at St. Louis, on a sailing ship equipped with oars. The two men went upriver into Indian territory, journeying through Oto, Omaha, Missouri, Sioux and Arikara, making contact with the Indians and noting the animals, plants, springs, paths and land.

When they reached Saskatchewan, a girl from the Shoshoni Tribe told them so much about what to expect that they decided to take her with them. And at the source of the Missouri River in the Rocky Mountains, the girl led them down the mountains, from river to river, until, on the 7th November 1805, Lewis and Clark saw the Pacific and the end of their long journey.

29 What is the "Check-In"?

When a person leaves for a journey by air, before boarding the aircraft, they have to go with their ticket to the Check-In Desk.

The ticket is divided into two parts. The person at the Check-In tears off one part and keeps it to put on their luggage, then gives the other part to the traveller. Free of luggage, the traveller can then go to board the aircraft, collecting his or her belongings when they reach their destination.

30 What is the Duty Free Shop?

The area occupied by an airport, like an aeroplane in flight, is considered to be "duty free" – that is, exempt from tax and customs duty. So, products sold at a Duty Free Shop inside an airport cost far less than shops outside.

Of course, the use of a Duty Free Shop is purely for passengers who have gone through the Check-In Desk – otherwise everyone would want to buy things there without paying tax or customs duty!

If, for any reason, a flight is delayed and passengers have to stay at the airport, they can take back whatever they have bought and get a refund.

The Duty Free Shop sells everything from clothes to chocolate and perfume.

The best things to buy are those where duty and tax makes them expensive – the difference in price can be quite remarkable.

But buying goods with low tax only weighs down luggage for the benefit of little saving.

31 What method of transport is the most extraordinary?

Imagination is the most extraordinary means of transport, also the most economic and versatile! Imagination took Jules Verne to the moon, beneath the oceans and around the world in eighty days, gave Emilio Salgari hair-raising adventures in the Indian jungle and enabled archaeologist Heinrich Schleimann to trace the heroes of Homer to Troy. And how many of us have gone to the Treasure Island which Stevenson wrote about?

SCIENCE AND TECHNOLOGY

Loading the Canoe

Loading the Canoe

"GET A MOVE ON, NIKKI!"

The man waiting by the loaded canoe was beginning to get impatient.

"Coming, Father!"

Fourteen year old Nikki hurried along carrying a magnificent jug, fine and delicate, decorated with grooves of wavy lines painted in black and a handle shaped like a bird.

"Isn't it lovely?" cried Nikki. "Mother makes beautiful pottery!"

He began helping his father with the loading of the canoe.

There were many other lovely jugs and pitchers which his mother had been busy making, and they all had to be packed most carefully among thick layers of leaves and grass, so that they would not get broken or damaged during the long journey.

When everything had been loaded, Nikki's father jumped on to the bank.

He made sure that the canoe was safely moored, then tied on a second, empty canoe to the stern of the first.

"We'll fill some stone jars with salted fish," he told his son. "Smoked fish, too. And we can take some cured meat for old Tapi to try. Our first batches have gone so well, I'm sure it will sell!"

The two set to work loading the second canoe, with men and boys working as they did all along the river.

Pitchers and stone jars full of fragrant honey, materials, quill pens, animal skins, bows and arrows... for a small village, it was clear that everyone had been very busy!

After a while, a lady came out of a pile dwelling on stilts and made her way to the bank, her violet-coloured tunic swaying as she walked.

Around her neck, discs of carved silver hung on a string of smooth leather, a huge bead of golden amber gleamed in the centre of a plaited leather rope, above a third necklace of beautiful shells.

"Take this one, too!" she said, holding out another pitcher – thin and light, with a beautiful swirling pattern and a handle made like a shell.

"Mother," breathed Nikki, "it – it's beautiful. All the village chiefs will want to buy it!"

"The necklace I asked for," he went on, "is it ready? You know, the one for Tapi's wife....."

His mother looked at him.

"For his wife?" she repeated, her eyes twinkling. "Or, his youngest daughter, perhaps?"

Nikki went red. "It's for his wife!" he insisted. "Tapi's daughter is a stupid baby, always laughing, and, and – "

"The necklace will be ready, anyway!" said his mother with a laugh. "But, Nikki – if it is for Tapi's wife, then why did you ask me to make it especially pretty?"

Nikki went redder than ever. He was glad when his father gave a shout from the second canoe, "How is the rest of the pottery going?"

"The first batch is almost ready!" said his wife. "But the second is still cooling off and I have left the third to drain. You'll be able to load the first two lots this evening, with the third at dawn tomorrow. But I'll need help to fire the last batch after sunset, otherwise I won't be able to sleep for worrying about the dew ruining the fresh clay!"

Nikki and his father nodded. "If we sell all the pottery," mother went on, "we could make another wheel and another kiln."

"We'll sell every piece!" her husband told her. "And I hope to get some flintstone tools which we need, in exchange. Then maybe you could try making a dagger from this new material, bronze... although I have heard it is rather dear to buy...."

"Will you bring me some nice material?" Nikki's mother said eagerly. "And find me a helper?" "A helper?" the man echoed. "Where will I find a woman who will want to come here?"

"Well, you can look around, anyway!" she smiled. "Why not try asking old Tapi? Didn't you say he's got a few daughters?"

"Hear that, Nikki?" said his father. "But you're always saying that Tapi's daughters are a load of babies!"

Nikki went as red as a beetroot, blushing to the roots of his hair, scraping at a twig with a flintstone.

His parents looked at each other. They knew that Nikki was no longer a a small boy. Perhaps Tapi's youngest daughter was no longer a baby in his eyes, either.

This story is just what could have happened in a European village around 3,500 years ago, when the supply pottery being made helped to develop business and relationships between different countries and groups of people.

1 What are frozen foods?

Very cold temperatures stop foods ripening and going bad. Fruits, green-stuffs, meats, cakes… foods stay frozen in the same state, as if no time has passed – rather like the Sleeping Beauty! When they are thawed, they begin to age, exposed to air and heat.

Fresh food is best frozen within half an hour at around 40 degrees below zero. It must be kept at very low temperatures to avoid being spoiled by partial thawing.

2 How does a refrigerator work?

A refrigerator works on the rule that liquids which evaporate become cold, and vapours which condense (return to liquid) become warm. The cooling down reduces heat and the condensation gives out heat.

In a refrigerator, we have a "chain" of evaporation and condensation. This "chain" takes place in a coil, which holds a special liquid. The coil is part inside, part outside the refrigerator.

Inside the refrigerator is the part in which the liquid evaporates, reducing heat, and outside, the part in which the liquid condenses, giving out heat, before flowing back into the part of the coil inside the refrigerator – and so the cycle goes on.

Opening the refrigerator too often means that heat gets in, making it carry out more cycles of evaporation/condensation, using up more electricity.

Refrigerators do not keep food as long as freezers, because their temperatures do not fall below zero.

3 How can we keep drinks hot?

The vacuum flask is a container which keeps drinks hot, consisting of three bottles – two inside have interiors which reflect back the heat given out. Separated by an empty space, these two bottles are both contained within a third, which has an insulated stopper to prevent the heat escaping through the outside.

So, the only way for the heat to get out is to unscrew the stopper of the flask!

4 When were tinned foods invented?

Tinned goods were invented in a European country renowned for food – France. In 1810 Nicholas Appert found a way of sterilising food in tin cans to keep for a long time.

His invention freed people from the problem of preserving food – until then, done by salting, keeping in brine or vinegar, smoking or drying, or in sugar. But the range of food which could be preserved was rather limited, and each method, apart from drying, changed the flavour of the food.

With Appert's invention, sterilisation of food in a sealed container did not change the flavour at all.

Tinned foods were not popular in France at first, but the invention was a great success in America. By 1860/70, their use began to spread, although Europeans were mistrustful for a long time, thinking that such foods would be tasteless and second-rate. But, of course, ideas gradually changed and people came to appreciate the value and convenience of tinned foods.

5 How does a microwave oven work?

In a microwave oven, there is a device called a magnetron.

The magnetron gives out a microwave beam – that is, a wave which has a strong heat capacity.

This micro-wave beam hits the fan at the top of the oven, which has silvery blades like a mirror – so that the wave reflects back to the walls of the oven, then bounces off on to the food, which is on a turntable to allow the microwave to reach every part.

Because the microwave shoots out and is then reflected back at a very high speed, the food cooks quickly, saving on electricity. The microwave oven is more economical than gas or electricity.

And how do plates and dishes stay cool enough to handle whilst the food is piping hot?

Well, unlike other types of oven, the microwave heats only the food and nothing else. This is because the microwave strikes the molecules of water found only in food – and these molecules move at very high speed, producing heat by their vibrating movement.

6 How is glass made?

Glass is made from combinations of many substances to produce various types. Ordinary bottle glass is made from silicon, aluminium, steel, calcium and sodium; crystal from silicon, lead and potassium.

The components are powdered and mixed in the right proportions then melted in ovens, before being refined to get rid of the air bubbles formed during the melting and finally made into objects by hand or machine.

7 When did metal-working begin?

Many metals can be worked in their natural state. Men soon discovered gold, silver, tin, lead and copper as tiny particles, nuggets or in seams underground, all of which could be beaten or melted and strained into moulds. 5,000 years ago, these metals were being worked in Egypt, India, China and Mesopotamia.

Then, men made bronze, using copper and tin – earliest bronzes date from around 3,500 years ago.

Steel did not appear until about 1,200 BC, due to difficulties in building up and keeping the high temperatures necessary for the work and to extract the slag which is in iron in its natural state.

When men began working as blacksmiths, they guarded the difficult techniques of the work – which is why they were so well paid.

In Europe, the best blacksmiths were the Celts, whose skill spread through Czechoslovakia, to Ireland and Spain, and the Etruscans, the men of central-northern Italy.

8 How do sundials work?

Sundials are solar clocks, based on the meridian line which represents the north to south direction of a place. This line is determined by the shortest shadow cast by a vertical arm on a background lit by the sun. The meridian line indicates mid-day, with other lines marking other hours.

Sundials were in use 6,000 years ago in Mesopotamia and Egypt. Many are still seen on the front of old buildings.

9 How do hour glasses work?

An hour glass is a clock which works on sand or water and made of two glass sections with a neck in between.

The sand or water flows from the upper section and by looking at the level of water in the upper or lower section, people had some idea of how much time had passed.

An hour glass contains the quantity of sand or water corresponding to a certain time – not always an actual hour!

10 When did clocks first appear?

A clock is any instrument which measures time – but the clock, as we know it, appeared only in the middle of the sixteenth century in the form of a pendulum clock.

Twenty years later, the balance wheel and hair-spring came into being for pocket watches.

From then on, the clock was continually improved upon until, by the end of the eighteenth century, the use and variety of clocks had increased still further.

In the sixteenth century, a clock-making industry was set up in Switzerland by French, Flemish and Italian refugees fleeing religious persecution. For over 500 years, Swiss clocks and watches have been renowned for their precision and reliability.

In the fifteenth century, people were woken up by the chimes of clocks in church towers or town halls.

And by the end of the sixteenth century, such a clock, working by weights and counter-weights, was the pride of any city; many had mechanical figures which beat the hours, often watched by crowds of admiring people!

Before then, people were roused from sleep by the sound of bells from churches or monasteries, which took their time from sundials scanning the seven divisions of the day.

And before then? There were only sundials and hour glasses, which were not very practical – the first because they could only work if there was sun, and the second because they were so often overturned.

11 Have there always been things made of rubber?

Gym shoes, balls, tyres... all things made from rubber are a present from America to Europe!

In the mid 1700's, men found that this vegetable product was both elastic and waterproof. So many uses were found, that men tried to make it artificially. But only in 1930 were satisfactory results obtained. Demand for rubber during the Second World War speeded up the process and now man-made rubber is widely used.

12 What are natural fibres?

Whether they are natural or man-made, textile fibres need to be long and soft, suitable to be spun into thread and then materials or plaited.

Natural textile fibres are obtained from animals, plants and minerals.

Sheep, camel, vicuna, alpaca, angora rabbits, cashmere goats... all give fine wool. Silk worms spin silk thread – and we get vegetable textile fibres from the coconut and cotton plant, from stems of the hemp plant, from broom, jute and flax, even the leaves of some plants.

The biggest world producer of wool is Australia, then Russia. China produces more than half of all the silk in the world, also taking first place for cotton, followed by the U.S.A. which also produces the most hemp, followed by India.

Russia produces the most linen, then comes China. Half the sisal in the world comes from Brazil, then Mexico. For jute, first place goes to India, second Bangladesh, with Greece for asbestos fibres.

13 How are artificial materials made?

Artificial materials are called "synthetic", because they are obtained from chemical synthetic compounds.

We can have either partly synthetic materials, or completely synthetic.

For wholly synthetic materials, compounds such as cellulose or protein are dissolved then passed through very thin holes, put in a special bath to remove the solvent, then put through again to form long threads.

14 How do we get energy from water?

From high in the hills, water flows down in rivers and falls on its way to the sea. This mass of movement can be used to generate energy to work a machine, with the water falling on to the blades of the wheel, making it turn. This wheel is connected to a machine like a mill wheel, grinding corn.

In ancient times, the use of hydraulic or water energy was not used very much. But from the Middle Ages onwards, it increased.

As well as grinding cereals, it went on to weaving, paper-making, metal-working and so on.

Then came the discovery of electricity and water came to be used to produce electrical energy in hydro-electric stations. Dams were built to create artificial lakes from which water fell on the turbines of a station at the foot of a dam.

Like the old water mills, when the water makes the turbines turn, they set the generator working which produces the electricity.

15 What is an atom?

An atom is the smallest particle in anything – solids, liquids, gases are all made up of atoms.

The simplest atom is of hydrogen. This looks rather like a miniature solar system, with a nucleus in place of the sun, a proton instead of a planet moving around the nucleus, and an electron.

Protons and electrons are found in equal numbers and by increasing protons, we get the various elements.

Two protons (and two electrons) is helium, three protons lithium – and so on, until we reach ninety two protons, which is uranium.

So everything around us and everything we use is made up of only ninety two elements.

Atoms join together to form a molecule. If they are all of the same element, then the molecule will be of that element. But where different atoms join, we get a molecule of a compound substance.

For example – a water molecule consists of two atoms of hydrogen and one of oxygen.

16 What is ecology?

The word "ecology" comes from two Greek words – "oikos" (ee-kos) meaning "home", and "logia", meaning study. So ecology is the study of our home, our surroundings or "environment" and the relationship between all living things and that environment.

In a house we need to consider the light, the type of floors, size of rooms, etc. before buying furniture.

So ecologists study the soil, climate, nature and any dangers which might threaten.

And, as in a house we use the space in a way where everyone feels the most comfortable, ecologists also study the best sites for buildings, so that people can feel at ease wherever they live.

Many laws and international organisations exist to safeguard nature and to promote sensible use of the environment. But no law can succeed without every one of us understanding that "home" is not only a space enclosed by four walls, but also the natural world which is outside it.

17 What is the type of energy given off by the sun?

On 15 August –"What is an atom?" – we read that adding protons to a nucleus makes a different element. But – where does the nucleus come from? Is it possible to join a nucleus with various elements?

Splitting a nucleus is called nuclear fission. Joining a nucleus to various elements, nuclear fusion. Both nuclear fission and nuclear fusion give out enormous amounts of energy. A simplified explanation can be found on 28 May, when we read about the sun. The energy given off by the sun is the result of nuclear fusion – the sun is the perfect nuclear fusion reactor!

More nuclear fission reactors are built than nuclear fusion reactors, but there are many risks. Nuclear fusion reactors are safer and cleaner, but have not yet been fully developed. One big problem is getting temperatures of at least 100,000,000 degrees per one fifth of a second – something which, until now, only the sun has managed without wearing out!

18 What is pollution?

The verb "to pollute" means to contaminate – for instance, with bacteria or harmful substances.

But in its wider sense, to pollute means to contaminate the natural environment, changing it to such an extent as to make it unfit for or harmful to living things.

Pollution of the environment is a harmful result of the activities of man.

The air becomes polluted with fumes from furnaces, factory chimneys and car exhaust fumes.

The earth becomes contaminated when it is polluted by non-biodegradable products in waste material.

Water becomes polluted with rubbish from homes and factories, and spillage from oil tankers.

The environment becomes polluted by bacteria and thoughtless use of chemical products.

There is also noise pollution which arises in certain places of work or in areas near airports, where the level of sound is above the tolerance threshold.

But although man has polluted the environment in the past, we are now beginning to understand that we have to use our brains a little, to think and to put things right as best we can.

When we all come to understand that the environment is actually our home, nobody will throw plastic bags in the sea, for example – because people will look upon the sea as their own, like the sides of their bath in the place where they live.

And who would want to throw plastic bags into their bath?

19 What is meant by "biodegradable"?

Anything that is biodegradable "degrades" or decomposes in a natural, biological way, through micro-organisms continually breaking down the matter, until it becomes carbon dioxide and goes back into the natural cycle.

An apple core, for example, will rot naturally. But only the outside of a battery can be broken down. The inside cannot rot, and so causes pollution. So, the apple core is bio-degradable. The battery is not.

20 How do we get energy from the wind?

Windmills are the best example of how to use energy from the wind!

They work in much the same way as water mills – but instead of a paddle wheel turned by water, the windmill has enormous sails pushed by the wind to make them turn.

We can use the wind to work machinery, and – in certain cases to produce electricity, too.

A windmill is built rather like a tower, and high up near the roof the wooden sails revolve on a huge spindle. When there is enough wind to drive the sails around, these turn a wheel inside the mill and this turns a vertical shaft. There are gears at the top and bottom of this shaft. Those at the bottom go into the "chests" or containers in which the cereals are broken up and ground into meal or flour.

Wind energy can be used only when the wind blows strongly for a good part of the year. The main advantage is that it is clean, free and inexhaustible. The disadvantage is that we cannot ask the wind to blow when we want it!

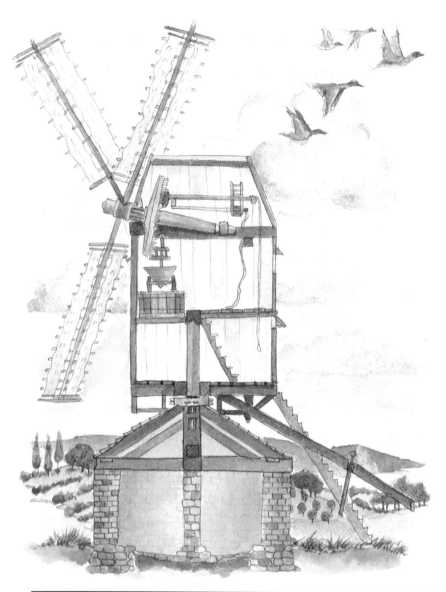

21 Which creatures warn us of pollution?

Trout are fussy enough to check the water where they live!

These fish live only in fresh, clean water in which there is a lot of oxygen.

If water becomes polluted, trout will make their escape in search of better conditions.

So, when trout start disappearing from a river, a stream or a lake, it is time to begin worrying.

But when they appear, this tells us that things are returning to normal.

Molluscs, on the other hand, such as oysters and mussels, are not affected at all by pollution.

This is why breeders of oysters and mussels keep a careful check on the waters where they live.

All the same, before enjoying a plate of mussels, it is always wise to ask the fishmonger or the cook about where they have come from. If you are not entirely happy with the answer, then change your choice of food.

With trout, there are no worries!

22 How can we preserve flowers?

Make a flower press! It is easy to do, using things you may have at home, or which can be bought cheaply.

First, decide on the size of the pressed flower pictures you want – whether these are going to be for an album, a picture, or whatever.

Then find two pieces of wood this size. On one piece of wood lay four or five sheets of folded newspaper, then some blotting paper or toilet tissue. Next, arrange the flower or plant exactly how you want it to look in the picture.

Then, on top of the plant, lay some more blotting paper or toilet tissue, then more folded newspapers and the second piece of wood and finally something heavy on top, such as a brick or large book – so that all moisture will be squeezed out of the flower.

It is best to change the newspapers and blotting paper or tissue every day until the plant is well dried. Then it is ready to be glued or fixed on to card, ready to go into an album, picture frame or whatever you prefer.

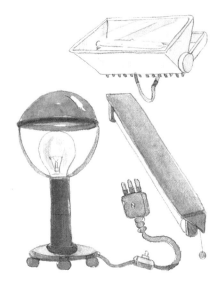

23 How does an electric lamp work?

There are many types of electric lamps – and in each one, electricity is used in slightly different ways to give us light.

In ordinary light bulbs, there is a filament through which runs an electric current, and when this glows it produces light.

If a filament is exposed to air, it will break in a moment – that is why it is enclosed in a glass bulb in which there is a vacuum or gas which will not make it burn out. This type of lamp gives out a warm light.

There is also a filament in a halogen lamp, but the bulb is a little cylinder of quartz in which there are vapours of a halogen chemical. This also gives a beautiful warm light. Halogen lamps are often used for car headlights.

Fluorescent lamps give out a whiter light, with gas flowing through a current.

This current stimulates the gas electrons which react by giving out light. The gases mostly used are neon, argon, sodium and mercury.

24 What is biological farming?

Biological farming uses only natural methods with the least amount of chemical products.

As well as natural fertilisers, biological farming also uses hedgehogs, toads and mayflies to destroy harmful insects, thrushes and centipedes to get rid of wireworms, and mint to keep at bay those insects which ruin bean crops.

Rows of carrots and onions criss-cross, because each protects the other from pests.

25 What is the bar code?

When we go shopping in big stores and supermarkets, we often see the cashier who, instead of tapping out the amount to pay on the keys of a cash register, rolls the striped square of each item across a glass viewer. This gives out a short bleep and the amount to pay appears on the cash register.

How does this happen? It is because the cashier has made a computer "read" the bar code on the product.

The little bars which we see are numbers in code, from which the name of the product is decoded.

When the cashier passes the bar code across the viewer, the computer reads it, then gives the price to the cash register.

But that is not all. In the memory of the computer, there is a list of the products on sale in the shop and the price for each item, showing the exact amount in stock at any given time – so when a product is sold out, it can tell the staff to re-stock the shelves.

26 What is a liquid crystal?

Liquid crystals are liquids but with molecules made like those of crystals.

Usually, these molecules are in no particular order. But when they receive a weak current of electricity they come together, blocking out light to appear opaque or letting light pass through and appearing transparent. With seven segments we obtain the numbers 0 – 9. By sending electrical signals, we show only some of the segments, which we read as numbers.

27 What types of artificial satellites are there?

Artificial satellites launched into space communicate with Earth by radio. Instruments on weather satellites send back images of the Earth with information for precise and up-to-date weather forecasts.

Communications satellites receive TV programmes and telephone messages from one part of the Earth and transmit them to another part. And astronomy satellites study space, sending back information to astronomers.

28 Where does technology come to the rescue of art?

At the end of the 1950's, Egypt resolved to build a dam on the Nile to make an artificial lake, which the country badly needed.

But as the waters of this man-made lake would cover the magnificent temples at Abu Simbel built to commemorate the Pharaoh Rameses and his Queen, UNESCO – the organisation of the United Nations for science and culture – decided that they should be dismantled and transferred to a safer place, so that Egyptians could preserve the artistic heritage of their ancestors.

This first example of archaeological team-work worldwide was a great success. Using the most advanced technological methods, it took four years for the temples to be transported 200 metres along the river and 65 metres higher up.

The cost was $40,000,000. But on 22 September 1968, when the "transplanted" temples were officially opened, nobody doubted that the money had been well spent.

29 What type of light is a laser beam?

Imagine a line of soldiers advancing with a steady, shuffling sound. When the commander orders, "Quick, March!" there is just one sound-wave, strong and loud. And if the soldiers could give out light, it would be a powerful light beam.

Well, the laser is a beam of lightwaves all the same frequency and coming from the same direction, so precise that it can be used in place of a surgeon's scalpel and so powerful that it can cut metal!

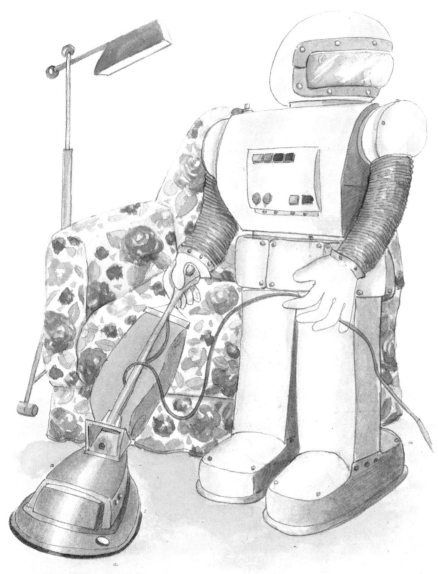

30 What can we use robots for?

Robots do not really look like the metal men which we imagine from seeing films and reading story books!

They are machines controlled by a computer, programmed to do the endlessly repetitive work which most people would find both tiring and boring. Also, robots can sometimes be programmed to work with substances and carry out jobs which may be dangerous to our health.

But only a computerised robot can "learn" to do such work instead of a person.

The memory of a computer remembers all the instructions which a programmer or operator supplies, so that it can give orders for the machine to do whatever the computer tells it.

For example, in the manufacture of cars, robot arms can be "trained" to spray on the paint from every angle.

And, who knows? Perhaps in the future, we may have a human-like robot who can speak, walk, think... just like those on the films and in the story books!

31 What is the difference between a computer and a calculator?

A calculator is a machine which is given a "memory" in which it can register the necessary instructions to complete a mathematical problem. This memory cannot be changed or added to. It consists of an "entry" where the user enters the numbers, a process which works out the mathematical operation, and a "unit of exit" where we see the result. That is the extent of the memory.

But instead of holding just one type of instruction in its memory at a time, a computer system can hold a series, called a programme.

Each programme tells the computer which series of instructions it must use to write, draw, paginate a book, plan a list of addresses, put names in alphabetical order, play games, read a bar code, send signals for the automatic function of machines, communicate with another computer to exchange information, etc.

The computer may do all a calculator can. But, not vice versa!

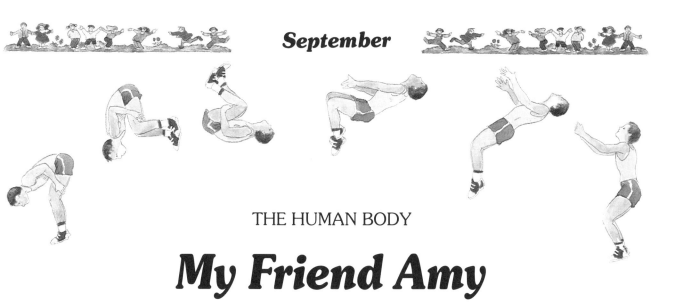

THE HUMAN BODY

My Friend Amy

My Friend Amy

IT WAS SUMMER TIME – but this year, Emma was not going on holiday.

Her father was so busy with his work and her mother did not want to leave him by himself.

"I don't want you working all day then coming home to an empty house!" she had said.

"You and Emma go!" Father had tried insisting. "I can always come down on Friday evenings to spend the weekend with you!" But Emma's mother had made up her mind.

And, Emma? She didn't mind very much!

Nearly every day, she met up with her friends at the swimming pool and then after tea they would go out again, meeting up with those who were coming back from holiday, saying goodbye to those who were leaving, going to band concerts and barbecues and picnics.

And when her friend Alice came to stay with her for a week, it seemed the summer was flying past.

Then, for a few days, Emma went to the swimming pool on her own.

One afternoon, she was drying herself in the sun after a nice swim, when she noticed a little girl she had not seen before. Her arms were tightly around her mother's neck as she carried her into the children's pool. She tried to get the little girl to swim, but it was no use.

Emma had to ask the lifeguard who they were.

He told her that the little girl, Amy, had been run over by a car quite a few months before and had spent a long time in hospital, where she nearly died.

She had then had some operations, and now the doctors said she had to have lots of exercise because her body was very weak after being in bed for so long.

Amy kept on saying that she could not move her legs – which was why her mother was bringing her to the swimming pool, hoping that, in the water, the little girl would get back the use of her legs.

"The water will keep you up!" Amy's mother was saying. "It will help you move your legs!"

"But my legs feel as if they are dead!" cried Amy. "I can't even stand up!"

After a while, Emma decided to go and make friends.

"Hello," she smiled, "my name's Emma. So now there's

two of us to help, one at either side!"

Amy looked up. And when Emma held out her hand, she slowly removed hers from around her mother's neck and held it tight.

"I'll get on my back," said Emma, "then you can get on top! Your mummy can hold both of us, then you can try to move with me!"

"Wonderful idea!" cried Amy's mother, glad of some help.

"You know, Emma, Amy is rather like a baby, learning to walk again!"

So Emma got in the water, holding Amy under her arms.

Gradually, and helped by Amy's mother, she began to let go, a little bit at a time.

Slowly, slowly, Amy relaxed and let go of Emma, too. And in a little while, she was floating with her!

Very gradually, they both began moving their arms together, staying like this for quite a while.

"All this work has made me feel hungry!" cried Emma at last. "I'm thirsty, too! Let's carry on afterwards, shall we?"

"I'm hungry, too!" cried Amy.

And without thinking, she turned around in the water, moving her legs a little!

Emma could see that her mother had noticed – but she said nothing, just led her towards the rail.

Over a fresh roll and orangeade, the two girls began talking.

"I come here every day!" said Emma. "If you like we can swim together again! Do you have any other friends who aren't away?"

"Y-yes." Amy faltered and took a sip of her orangeade. "But – well, I know I hold them back."

"That's being a bit selfish!" Emma burst out. "Your friends must like you a lot. How do you think they feel when they want to do all they can for you, and you won't let them?"

"Oh!" exclaimed Amy, taken aback. "I – I hadn't thought of that!"

"We could start by going out for an ice cream!" Emma went on, quite enjoying herself. "Will you do something for me?"

Amy nodded, beginning to smile.

"Well, telephone one of them, then telephone me, and we'll all meet up. You'll see what we can do between us!"

"How about inviting me, as well?" smiled the lifeguard. "I wouldn't mind going out for an ice cream, myself!"

1 What is the human body made of?

The human body is a complex mechanism! It is made up of millions of cells which in turn make up over 200 bones, more than 600 muscles, 6 metres of intestines, etc. It can carry out a wide range of different activities, from carrying a heavy load, to working with the finest gold leaf; from looking into the universe, to finding out more about how the body works.

No other living thing has a body so complex.

2 How has man changed over thousands of years?

According to the theory of evolution, millions of years ago, there were many types of ape, each one different from the other but all belonging to the family of primates.

It was from this family, or species, that man descended.

Long before even prehistoric times, our ancestors lived in trees, together with the apes from whom they were descended, and adapted to life on earth by learning to walk upright.

In fact, man is the only primate who stands upright – because our bones are different to those of other primates in allowing us to straighten up.

This ability to stand on one's feet offered man the unique opportunity of having his hands free.

Man's hands have a thumb, the same as other primates.

Once man no longer needed his hands for help in walking, he began to adapt them for other uses. Soon he started to make things such as simple tools and weapons from wood and flintstone.

3 What use is sport?

To exercise the muscles properly, the heart has to pump harder and so we breathe faster – and the oxygen goes to all parts of our body, not only those which are actually involved in the exercise.

That is why, when we run, we get healthy, pink cheeks.

The brain works better, too. So, if a person has been studying too much and finds it difficult to concentrate, a run out in the open air will refresh them.

4 What are vitamins?

Vitamins are substances necessary for the development and health of the body.

They are found in almost all foods and any deficiency brings about various problems.

A shortage of Vitamin A, for example, causes problems with the eyes and in the growth of bones and teeth. A shortage of Vitamin B, loss of weight, dryness of the skin and mouth sores; and a scarcity of Vitamin D hinders the formation of bones.

So the way to avoid problems is to keep to a balanced diet, which includes lots of fruit and fresh green vegetables – cooking, and using preservatives and additives makes many vitamins disappear.

Going out in the open air as much as possible in fine weather is also very good, because sunshine "fixes" calcium in bones.

The times when we run the greatest risk of illness – in winter, for example, it is wise to eat more of the things containing Vitamin C – citrus fruits, cabbages, potatoes to help the body defend itself.

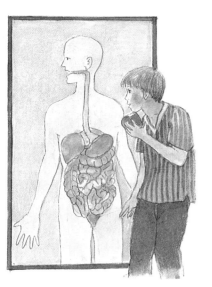

5 Why do we need to eat?

All the cells of our body work hard, constantly being renewed to make up our tissues, our bones, blood, etc. To be able to work, the cells need a special type of sugar, called glucose, which is brought to them through the blood.

The blood gets glucose from the liver which gives out its supply very, very slowly, wherever it is needed.

In turn, the liver gets blood through an artery and a vein.

The artery brings the liver the blood which gives it the energy to work, and the vein brings it enriched blood from the small intestine, where, as a result of everything we eat, digestion is finally completed.

So from all the food that we eat, the liver stores glucose until it is needed in whatever part of the body.

Whatever part of the food not needed after digestion is either filtered out by the kidneys or passes into the large intestine, ready to be emptied by the body.

131

6 What is a diet?

When people talk about "going on a diet" they usually mean they are trying to slim.

In fact, diet refers to sensible nutrition for a variety of purposes – to gain, as well as to lose weight, for the physical strain of the sportsman, the mental strain of the student, for the person who is an employer, a mountain guide, someone suffering from stomach troubles, a diet to counteract summer heat or winter cold, etc.

7 How many senses do we have?

We have five senses – touch, taste, smell, sight and hearing.

The sense of touch is through the skin, by which we recognise the shape and temperature of an object and the material from which it is made.

The palm of a hand, the sole of a foot and the forehead are the most sensitive parts of the body; the leg is one of the least sensitive.

Most people's noses can identify the least of chemical substances in the air.

The tip of the tongue identifies sweet tastes; the back, bitter tastes, the side edges acid and the centre salt.

In the case of sight, the eyelids protect the eyes from intense light and moving them helps keep particles out of the eye. Eyelids and eyebrows do the same job.

Tear ducts keep the inside of the eyelids moist.

And our ears?

They give us not only our hearing and perception of sound but also our balance.

8 What is the best weight / height?

To decide on the best weight for any height, we have to decide whether a person has long limbs, normal limbs (in proportion to the trunk) or short limbs. Thus, a boy of 11 years old and 1.40 metres tall should weigh 34 kilos, whereas a girl of the same age and 1.43 metres high should be 37 kilos. At 15 years old, a boy 1.62 metres tall should weigh 53 kilos and a girl with a height of 1.58 metres should weigh 51 kilos.

9 What happens when we are frightened?

We are going along a street, when a dog suddenly barks at us. If we are not used to animals, it will be difficult to be quite calm about it.

More probably, we shall be frightened and stop in fear.

After a second, though, we may shout or try to control ourselves, perhaps go up to the dog, waiting for the next movement, wondering how we shall defend ourselves.

But in that fraction of a second, our body reacts, too. Our eyes and ears send back to the brain an image of the dog and its barking.

The brain identifies the message as a danger and releases a hormone called adrenalin to increase the glucose content in the blood, ready to give the muscles extra energy.

As well as this, the adrenalin increases the heartbeat and quickness of breath. So, the body has muscular energy to escape, breath to shout, the strength to wait without moving. And all this has happened so fast that our reaction is immediate.

10 What are psycho-somatic illnesses?

As a human body in good shape helps the brain to work better, so mental health can influence the body.

The mind (psyche) and body (soma) depend on each other – so mental stress can have repercussions on the body, making it ill.

Such illnesses are called psycho-somatic. These can include ulcers, migraine, gastritis, fatigue and other illnesses caused in some degree by mental stress.

And until the mental cause of the illness is dealt with, a cure will be difficult, if not impossible.

For instance – suppose a boy is unhappy at school. He has mental strain in trying to study things which do not interest him and poor marks only make him feel worse. He sleeps badly, so is irritable and listless in the morning.

In turn, all this means that he cannot digest his food and he gets a headache.

His mental condition is communicated to the body, which reacts with feelings of illness.

11 What are bio-rhythms?

Who jumps out of bed bursting with energy – and who gets up somewhere around nine o'clock? Who can study up to midnight – and who wants to go to bed early, tired out?

Each day, we all have peak times of physical and mental energy and times when these are at their lowest. To discover our own cycle of productivity – bio-rhythms – there are special tables so that we see when they occur and plan our work around them.

12 Why do we need blood tests?

By analysing a blood sample, we can discover so much. Blood consists of many elements which must be in certain quantities and have a particular appearance. Any alteration in these elements can tell us what is happening in the body.

For example, a high number of white corpuscles is a sign of infection, because these are the "guards" of the body – whenever any kind of attack takes place, the body produces lots more white corpuscles to defend itself.

As well as the composition of blood, a blood test looks at many other things – if there is a virus or bacteria present, for instance.

Blood tests are the bases for a doctor to discover what a person is suffering from.

Often this information is only to "explore" the body. Sometimes other tests are needed, such as cardiographs, x-rays or magnetic resonance imaging.

But usually, the information which a doctor receives from this is enough for a diagnosis to be made and a cure decided upon.

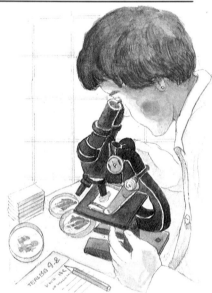

13 What is the purpose of vaccination?

When a body is attacked by poisons or "toxins", it defends itself by producing anti-toxins – but this takes time.

Vaccination introduces into the body a tiny quantity of toxins to get the body to produce anti-bodies – it gives the body a slight attack of the illness, in order to fight it, putting the body in a position to defend itself from the illness in the event of a serious attack at sometime in the future.

14 What do white corpuscles do?

Blood is made up of red corpuscles which carry oxygen and white corpuscles which defend the body against outside "enemies".

White corpuscles are "soldiers", always ready to fight; if the body is attacked, they rush up to destroy the bacteria. The outward sign of battle is the pus, made up mostly of white corpuscles "dead" in battle; so when pus appears, you know that the body is able to fight its enemies!

15 What is "a temperature"?

Our normal body temperature ranges between 36.5 and 37 degrees centigrade.

Many illnesses can make the temperature rise above 37 degrees, and this is called "a temperature".

It is not an illness in itself, but a sign that the body is being attacked by illness, defending itself by increasing its normal temperature.

Apart from a rise in body temperature, breathing will be faster and the heartbeat accelerated.

With a temperature, the doctor will try to decide what caused it and how to cure the illness. Then, the high temperature will go along with the illness.

So, taking pills does not lower a high temperature. What this will do is to soothe and quieten the body, to help it fight the enemy.

The temperature itself and how it rises and falls gives the doctor valuable information to understand what the illness was which caused it and to decide on the best cure.

16 What are tears?

Tears are produced by the tear-ducts situated under the upper eyelid. Tears flow down the lower eyelid towards the nose, where they collect – which is why, when we cry, we need to blow our noses.

Tears protect the eye. If it is irritated by strong light, wind, smoke, or if a gnat, or speck of dust gets into the eye, tears are produced in a greater quantity than usual, and in crying, help rinse away the irritation.

135

17 What is the use of x-rays?

By sending an electrical current through a special tube, we produce radiation – rays which can go through matter.

In the case of x-rays, a photographic plate is put behind the part of the body being "hit" by the rays.

That way, we can see the parts they have been unable to pass through – and so we get a photograph of the part to be examined, ready to be interpreted by the radiologist.

18 What do antibiotics do?

Antibiotics is a term used for medicines produced by living organisms – certain bacteria and specially-grown "cultures" – which fight against other bacteria and viruses.

As antibiotics are very powerful medicines, they must be taken exactly as prescribed by the doctor.

The discovery of antibiotics is fairly recent. In 1932, Scottish doctor, Alexander Fleming, noticed that germs which he was studying had been accidentally destroyed by some mould.

His research as to why this happened led to the discovery of penicillin, which has saved millions of lives.

And as projects and studies have increased, so have antibiotics, reducing the spread of serious illnesses such as meningitis, typhoid, whooping cough, diphtheria, tuberculosis and many others.

Antibiotics are also used for animals and plants in fighting diseases which destroy breeding and culture, reducing hunger over vast regions of the Earth.

19 Why do we need to brush our teeth?

We use our teeth to break up food so that it can pass into the stomach.

Some pieces of food remain trapped between the teeth and, because of our saliva, it decomposes very quickly.

This decomposition forms a solid plaque, which attacks the gums as well as the teeth themselves.

So, a thorough cleaning of teeth after every meal prevents plaque forming.

20 Why does the sun burn more in the mountains?

The mountain air is much purer than at sea level. So, the sun's rays have to pass through a much thinner layer, thus hitting with a much greater force. When the sun is reflected in the snow and ice, this force increases, and it can cause eye problems when people do not wear dark glasses. Here, they need to protect themselves from the sun more than by the sea, especially in the winter when it is easiest of all to get sunburn.

21 Is it good for us to get brown?

Tanning is a sign that the skin is defending itself – so the idea of feeling better physically when we have a nice sun tan is only in the mind, because it makes us look better.

Being on holiday and resting more means that we tan faster, but suntan by itself does not improve a person's health.

The sun does us good by setting or "fixing" the calcium in our bones, and the sea air is very healthy because it is rich in iodine.

But it is not wise to spend the days lying in the sun without doing anything.

Far better to move around, go walking, swimming, to play and stay in the shade during the hottest part of the day to get the best from a stay by the sea or in the mountains.

Soreness and sunburn are a result of too much exposure to the rays of the sun which can be avoided by wearing a hat, a light dress or T-shirt and moving around, so that the tan comes naturally.

22 What is "mountain sickness"?

If in the mountains, a person complains of buzzing in the ears, feeling tired and dizzy – that is mountain sickness. The higher we go above sea level, the purer the air.

So in the mountains, breathing normally takes less oxygen into the lungs and the body reacts. The sufferer must rest, and if the sickness does not pass, descend to a lower height, going up again slowly, so that the body gets used to the air.

23 How do we go underwater?

The higher we go up, the more the air pressure decreases. The deeper we go down, the more it increases.

Our body is used to the air pressure at sea level, so we must allow it to get used to a different air pressure.

Underwater, we need to go down slowly, just as we have to rise up again slowly, to give the body time to adjust to the large increase and reduction in pressure.

24 Why do we put a broken limb in plaster?

When we break an object, we spread a little glue on the two surfaces where the break has occurred, fit it together, then protect the two parts until the glue is dry.

We do the same sort of thing – but without the glue – with a broken bone.

First, the doctor will arrange for an x-ray of the injured limb and see if the break (or fracture) is across, length-ways or a cross-break and if there are any chips, bone splinters, or other complications.

Then, after bringing the two edges of the broken bone together to set, the bone must be made to keep quite still, with a bandage and a splint, or a plaster cast.

The "glue" will be made by the bone itself, as it produces bony material called "callus" over the broken area to allow it to heal.

The time this takes varies according to the break and the bones involved – from a few weeks for a forearm to months for a pelvis or a broken leg.

25 What makes swimming the perfect sport?

Of all sports, swimming is the one which brings into play all the muscles in the human body.

As well as this, moving in the water helps us to get a perfect balance between the left and right sides of the body, improving our co-ordination – the way the different parts of our body work together.

This is why swimming is ideal for people who need to get back the use of a part of the body weakened for any reason.

26 Why do people need glasses?

When we use a camera, the image of an object is focused on the lens which is produced upside-down and reduced on to the film.

With the eye, the lens is the pupil and the film is the retina. When an object is "in focus" – that is, seen clearly – the image is formed on the retina.

If the image is behind the retina, that is long-sightedness, where a person sees best the things which are furthest away.

If the image is in front of the retina, that is short-sightedness, where a person needs to have things close to be able to see them clearly.

Just as a photographer would adjust his camera, so an optician carries out tests and finds the best lenses to enable a person to focus an image on the retina.

Many people wear glasses for reading, drawing, studying, watching television, computer work and driving.

Any artificial light alters the elasticity of the eye and its ability to focus.

27 What can we see if we are colour blind?

When a bullfighter waves his red cape in front of the bull, people think the colour red makes the animal angry.

In fact, the bull sees the world in black and white.

It seems that this applies to all mammals, except primates – apes and man. Birds, reptiles, fish and insects also see colours, whereas we think that cats and dogs, bears and cows, whales and seals and so on, do not see colour.

But not everyone can see all the colours. Some of us cannot make out colours properly, and some can distinguish only some – usually green and red. These people are affected by colour blindness, an abnormality first studied by John Dalton, who was himself afflicted. That is why the medical name for colour blindness is Daltonism.

We still do not understand why it happens.

What we do know is that it is something to do with the 7,000,000 "cones" in the eye, which actually receive the colours, and around 120,000,000 "rods" taking in the light rays.

28 What is the best way to sit?

Our spinal column is not straight and closely packed together.

It is a series of bones or vertebrae arranged in a column which goes into two curves, at shoulder level and at the waist.

The vertebrae can turn in all directions, allowing us more freedom of movement than any other living thing.

So, the spinal column must be treated with respect – not by sitting at a table with the head resting on an arm, stooping or leaning forward, pushing against the spinal vertebrae.

Treatment like this can cause permanent damage – such as the spine "leaning" to the left or right; a continually bent back can cause a curved spine, and constant strain on the lower vertebrae can bring about lumbar problems.

All these painful injuries can easily be avoided, by sitting upright with the spine well supported, not sitting too long in one position and getting up to stretch the limbs after sitting for any length of time.

29 What is meant by something being "anatomical"?

Anatomy is the science which studies the form and structure of living things.

There are "anatomical" chairs with adjustable height, having shoulder rests which support the spinal column correctly and with no bulging edges to obstruct the circulation of the blood, etc.

Numerous objects, from stairs, to beds, to armchairs, take account of the human anatomy and the well-being of the human body.

30 What is sleep?

Sleep is a temporary lapse of consciousness. When we sleep, the central nervous system slows down, also slowing down our breathing, heart-beat, muscle-tone, and so on.

The time when we sleep and the number of hours necessary varies enormously. Babies sleep 18 – 20 hours a day; young children 12 – 14 hours, adults 7 – 9 and older people 5 – 7 hours.

Many people sleep more or less than average, or spread the total number of hours at different times for example, six hours at night and one during the day.

Difficulty in sleeping is called insomnia, where people cannot help getting up early or find it quite impossible to sleep.

Although it is not an illness, insomnia is a physical disturbance which can be caused by anxiety, depression, excitement.

It cannot be cured without getting rid of the problems which cause it. But temporary insomnia can be overcome by drinking camomile tea.

FOOD AND DRINK

My Friend the Wolf

My Friend the Wolf

STEFAN LOOKED around at the birch and fir trees which surrounded him.

There was not much grass, and snow had fallen much earlier than usual this year.

How topsy-turvy the seasons seemed to be just lately, Stefan thought to himself!

Still, at least his sheep had enough to eat, and there was a warm fire burning in the middle of the forest clearing.

Stefan picked up his axe and went to chop some wood, ready to keep it going through the night. A fire was the only defence he had to keep wild animals from eating his sheep.

It had been a hard year so far. The harvest had failed, so the grass had not lasted in the pastures. Even the birds had migrated earlier than usual.

Stefan turned his thoughts to his father who had left two moons ago to find new land where they could live a little better.

With so many people now living in the village, there was not enough food for everyone. So, he had sailed off with another twenty warriors.

Like the rest of the village women, his mother was doing her best to grow food and tend the earth.

Boys like him either looked after the sheep, caught fish or hunted whatever game still remained.

Sighing a little, Stefan went to see if he had caught anything in the traps he had set earlier on, among the beech trees.

They were all empty. So he decided, he would have to be content with just milk.

He was only thankful that he had plenty of wood for the fire – that, and a hole dug in the earth and covered with branches was enough to keep him from feeling cold.

It would be a still night, Stefan thought, beginning to feel drowsy.

He did not know how long he slept, before being awoken by loud bleating.

Clutching his knife, he reached out his other hand to grasp a flaming branch, holding it up to give him enough light to look around his flock.

True, they seemed disturbed – and yet he could see no reason for it. In the end, he put some more wood on the fire and went

back to sleep.

But before very long, the sheep began bleating again, louder this time. Once more, Stefan picked up a flaming branch. And as he looked around, he saw some prints in the snow – the footprints of a wolf, probably only a cub , he guessed – and a wolf cub was not really a danger.

Next day, Stefan was pleased to find a big bird in one of his traps. Some feast that would make, he thought, roasted over the fire!

The following night passed quietly, until daybreak when the sheep awoke, bleating as usual.

And this time when Stefan got up, he saw that the wolf cub's prints were near the remains of his meal, every morsel of meat stripped from the bones until they were completely bare.

"He must have been hungry!" Stefan said to himself. "I wonder if he's lost his mother? Maybe if I give it some milk and a few bones, that will keep him away from my lambs...."

The wolf cub could not resist a nice bowl of fresh milk! Stefan watched him coming nearer, lapping the milk greedily then gnawing the bones. He was very young, as Stefan had guessed.

After that, he prepared something for the wolf cub every evening, watching it eat and then going away – until one night when it settled down near the bowl and went to sleep.... Stefan was pleased!

Next night, he put the cub's food a little nearer the fire. Once again, the wolf ate, then went to sleep until dawn. And so it continued. And each night, Stefan felt happier, the sheep were less disturbed and the wolf more trusting.

"Tonight," the boy announced to the birch trees, "I'll have him eating out of my hand!"

When the time came, he sat near the bowl of milk and threw some meat to the wolf cub, closer and closer, until, at last, he held a piece in his hand!

The wolf cub crept forward, sniffed the food – and ate it! He let Stefan stroke him too, and when the boy settled down to sleep by the fire, the wolf cub curled up beside him.

The story of Stefan, a boy who probably lived somewhere around 200 or 300 A.D., is the tale of an age-old trust which gave man his most faithful friend – the dog.

1 What food did prehistoric man eat?

We can get some idea of how our ancient ancestors lived by seeing how some people live today.

The Australian Aborigines and the Amazon Indians of South America, for example, do not farm the land nor do they breed cattle. Instead, they hunt and they fish, knowing the likely places where they can gather fruit, roots, seeds, shoots, leaves and flowers, using bark and wood for the things they need.

They keep in groups, eating little by little of whatever food they can find or catch. And when a place can offer them no more, they simply move on.

So it was with prehistoric men. For thousands of years they could not produce their own food, but relied on nature and whatever was "given" by animals.

But as they watched and learned, they began making traps to catch the mammoth, the sabre-toothed tiger and the bear. And they taught themselves to do things such as using a stone to sharpen a stake and to weave materials.

2 When did man first begin to cook food?

Let us go back five hundred thousand years to a cave near Bejing where a Chinese family sat eating around the fire.

When a little boy dropped his piece of raw meat into the fire, how his mother scolded him! Food was scarce during the winter.

Then Father gave the boy his piece, cursing a little as he poked a stick into the fire to get the sizzling meat.

Then, he took a bite. And how good it tasted!

This may be only a story – but both the place and the time have been verified by archaeologists.

Whether there really was a little boy who dropped his meat into the fire, we shall never know.

But once people discovered how good roasted meat tasted, they soon began to prefer it that way instead of eating it raw!

They cooked it on embers, roasted it over the fire on sticks or used stone slabs or tripods of wood on which they threaded or hung the meat to be cooked.

3 How did prehistoric man catch the woolly mammoth?

The woolly mammoth was a huge animal, rather like our elephant, but with thick fur and long, curved tusks.

To capture it, men threw lots of pointed sticks, clubs made of bone or stone or flint knives.

They also needed lots of patience and cunning!

Mammoth hunters had to work in groups. One man would find it too difficult to kill a mammoth. And even if he did, it would be too big a job to skin it and cut it up.

So once snow fell, groups of hunters would gather together. When they saw a mammoth, they would surround it, making it back away towards a swamp, ravine or a deep hole which they had dug.

Once the beast had fallen in, they would attack it with lances and catapults, waiting patiently until it died of hunger or its wounds.

Then all the people would gather around to help skin and cut the mammoth up. There would be enough food for a long time! And as well as meat, they would use the mammoth's fur to make clothes and shoes, blankets and curtains. And with the tusks and bones they would make weapons, frames for the curtains and so on.

The meat was buried in the snow to prevent it from going bad and eaten gradually.

Once it was finished, the tribe would go off in search of another mammoth, bison, rhinoceros or deer.

Even today, Eskimos at the North Pole live and hunt in a similar way.

4 How did prehistoric man catch birds?

Prehistoric man did not have bows and arrows to catch birds. So, he aimed sharp stones at them wherever they gathered. Or he might attract them with seed and then throw a net over them.

Sometimes, too, he would throw a handful of seeds on the ground, then put down some stakes covered with sticky resin from the trees. Then he would watch for the birds to come down for the seeds and get caught between the stakes.

5 How did prehistoric man catch fish?

By keeping still near the water, prehistoric man waited until fish drew near, then threw either a pointed stick or a javelin, or simply hit the fish with a stick. And whenever he saw fish leaping, he would simply catch them as they jumped out of the water.

Another method was to put a trellis of wood as a barrier in a stream. Once fish were clustered behind it, they would put another trellis in front and capture them.

6 Which fruit and vegetables were there in prehistoric times?

Fruit and vegetables were different in prehistoric times to what they are now.

But we can get some idea of this difference when we go into country or mountain areas and find sour-tasting wild plums only as big as cherries and small, bitter apples.

Blackberries, currants, raspberries, grapes, strawberries, hazelnuts, almonds, walnuts, chestnuts... all these were the same. But pears, apricots, cherries and peaches were smaller and not so sweet. Fruits such as bananas, melons, pineapple and coconut were found only in the tropics.

Mushrooms, broad beans, chicory and herbs, cabbages and carrots, beet and celery... these were all much the same as today. Then there were wild-growing cereals such as wheat, barley and rye.

With these, Prehistoric man made soup, in much the same way as the North American Indians do today, with no cooking pots or metal utensils.

Instead, they use their spades to make tripods, ready to hold strong leather containers full of water with vegetables and perhaps pieces of meat or fish.

Then with branches of trees made into a kind of fork, they would take a red-hot stone from the fire and plunge it into the water, so that it would boil up to make a soup.

Another way was to dig a hole and line it with a skin kept in place with stones around the edge, then filling this with water, vegetables and red-hot stones.

7 What animals did men first breed?

It is easy to see why the first animals bred by man were sheep and goats. As well as giving milk and wool, they were easy to look after as they grazed. Then they went on to pigs – still wild at this time, but very useful because every part could be eaten, giving excellent meat. After that came cattle, which needed more care and better shelter. But in the work of breeding as well as hunting, man had a wonderful helper – the dog.

8 Where did farming begin?

In an area between Turkey, Iran and Palestine, around 8000 B.C. men began planting seeds of corn and barley which they took from adult plants, watered, grew and then harvested. And with the cultivation of plants for food, they became growers as well as animal breeders.

With these skills, men were able to produce their own food.

No longer did they have to move around following migrating animals, so they built shelters, stables and proper homes. Weaving and pottery developed and better weapons and tools were made.

To appreciate how important all this was, it is worth remembering that the oldest remains of man that have been found so far were three million years old.

From then until only ten thousand years ago, man depended entirely on what nature gave him.

And now, ten thousand years later, man is journeying into space.

9 How can we keep foods today?

From ancient methods of keeping food, such as freezing, salting, smoking or keeping in brine or sugar, we get modern methods of keeping food in tins and freezers, which we read about during August. But there are still more – for example, the freeze-dry method, where food is dehydrated, and the pasteuriser in which heat neutralises germs. As well as keeping food, such methods also keep the ascorbic acid or Vitamin C content.

10 Is coffee good or bad for you?

Coffee contains caffeine, a substance which stimulates the heart and nervous system. So it is easy to see that too much coffee is not good. How much coffee to drink is for each person to decide – but drinking coffee late at night, especially before going to bed means a sleepless night. Adding milk simply means a diluted coffee.

Like coffee, tea also contains caffeine, and so has the same effect.

11 What exactly is jam?

Fruit can be preserved in alcohol or syrup. It can be candied – or changed into jelly, or jam. So, jam is a way of preserving fruit!

People were making quince jelly and lemon juices before the 15th century. Then cane sugar and candied fruit began arriving from India. And by the 18th century, when people began getting sugar from sugar beet, jam was made at home.

The manufacture of jam in factories began only after the invention of tinned foods.

Before that, jam could only be made by people who had lots of ripe fruit – those living in the country or who had big gardens.

In many stories from the 18th century to the beginning of the 20th, we read of children taking jam from larders, which shows that jam was a treat, to be enjoyed sparingly.

There are many types of jam – each fruit cooks differently, and also most regions and countries have their own traditions and recipes for jam-making.

12 What are "St. James' shells"?

In the Middle Ages, people went on pilgrimages to the centres of Christianity – Rome, Jerusalem.... and to the shrine of St. James of Compostela in Spain, one of the most famous and popular shrines.

Pilgrims who went to Compostela were always given a special shell, with which to ask for alms.

These were those of *Pecten Jacobaeus* – delicious-tasting scallops which so many people enjoy today.

148

13 When was rice first grown?

Archaeologists have found remains of rice dating from 1700 B.C. in the valley of the Indus in India – but we know that it was being grown before then in countries such as China and Indonesia, where it was popular from ancient times.

Rice was known to the Ancient Greeks and Romans, but they did not use it. Instead, it was the Arabs who introduced rice-growing to Europe when they invaded Spain in the 8th Century.

14 Which types of foods come from animals?

Foods contain various quantities of three main elements – carbohydrates, fats and protein – as well as vitamins and minerals, substances which our bodies need, but cannot produce.

Carbohydrates and fats are used by the body as sources of energy. Protein is used mainly for body-building and renewing body tissue. Vitamins work in different ways and mineral salts are necessary for numerous bodily functions.

Food from animals include – meat, fish, butter, lard, eggs, cheese and milk which provide different levels of these elements. For example, butter usually contains fat, but little carbohydrate or protein; rabbit meat is rich in protein but low in carbohydrate and fat; Emmenthal cheese contains about the same quantity of protein and fat, but lacks carbohydrate; eggs are rich in protein and fats but low in carbohydrate – and full cream milk contains all three food elements in roughly equal measure.

15 Which types of food do we get from vegetables?

Like the foods we get from animals, vegetable foods also contain carbohydrate, fats, protein, vitamins and minerals.

Some examples – potatoes are rich in carbohydrate, poor in fat and protein; coconut is high in fat, low in protein; beans are high in carbohydrate and protein, low in fat. Olive oil is solely fat. Jams are rich in carbohydrate, low in fat. Chocolate is rich in fat and carbohydrate, but poor in protein.

16 When did people begin making bread?

Bread is made mainly from flour and water. Yeast and salt are used in most breads, but not all.

Bread is easy to make and our farming ancestors soon learned the knack.

But for a long time they did not know of yeast, so they made flat bread, pancakes and types of biscuit which could be cooked on hot stone.

Then, around three thousand five years ago, the use of yeast was discovered in Egypt.

Easy and cheap to make.... it is not surprising that bread became the basic food for most countries.

In Ancient Rome, there were even public ovens controlled by magistrates and many a revolt in times of hardship has been sparked off by the cry of "Bread!" – such as the French Revolution.

There are sayings about bread in most languages, too – and, of course, many of us say "Give us this day, our daily bread," in prayer.

In olden times, white bread enriched with oil or butter was a symbol of wealth, whilst bread made from different flours – corn, wheat, barley, rye – was a sign of poverty – unlike today, when such bread is extremely popular, not only due to its taste, but because we also know how good and nourishing it is in any diet.

Nowadays, we can buy bread containing olives, onion, garlic, herbs... bread-sticks and biscuits, as well as sweet-flavoured bread.

Ancient Egyptians, too, could choose from around five hundred different types, and their earth ovens baked over one hundred and forty sorts of loaf!

17 When was the pizza invented?

The pizza began in Naples, Italy, as a dish for poor people. At first, they were made of bread with cheese, basil, salt and pepper. Tomatoes were added only after the discovery of America, and pizzas were made long before that – precisely when, nobody knows.

But, as the pizza is known throughout the world as a dish with tomatoes, perhaps it is more correct to look upon it as an Italian-American invention!

18 Where was the hamburger invented?

Whoever thinks that the hamburger was born in America and came to Europe in recent times is mistaken! As the name suggests, Hamburg in Germany gave its name to this flat cake of minced meat cooked on a grill or a hot-plate. From Germany, the hamburger went to America, where it became famous before coming back to Europe along with American "French Fries".

Another food which originally came from Germany is the frankfurter, the sausage made from finely chopped meat put into a soft skin. And although there is a similar sausage coming from Vienna in Austria, it is after the town of Frankfurt that they are named.

Hamburgers and frankfurters are very tasty with ketchup – tomato sauce spiced in a number of different ways. The name may be English – but ketchup originally came from Malaya!

Some people prefer mayonnaise – and this delicious concoction of egg, oil, salt and vinegar or lemon juice was first mixed in France.

19 How many types of sweeteners are there?

There are both natural and artificial sweeteners.

The first used by man was honey, then came cane sugar and sugar beet, sugar in fruits and lactose in milk.

But as well as sugar cane and sugar beet, sugar is present in many plants, too. In North America, for example, the Indians extract a syrupy liquid from the trunk of a type of Maple tree. This is called Maple Syrup, whilst the Latin name for the tree is *Acer saccharinum* – Sweet Maple. Maple Syrup was much appreciated by Europeans who emigrated to America, and today is widely used in the food industry.

Artificial sweeteners are produced in laboratories for certain purposes – to sweeten medicines or drinks or in special diets where sugar is forbidden. Saccharin, 500 times more powerful than natural sugar, permits the sweetening of food whilst helping to reduce the amount of sugar taken in by the body.

20 Why do we use herbs in cooking?

We use herbs not only to improve the flavour of food, but also for the many good qualities they have.

Rosemary is a tonic and basil is a sedative. Sage strengthens the gums and is a disinfectant, along with mint and rue which also aid digestion. Parsley contains iron, phosphorous and calcium, as well as Vitamins A and C – just five grammes gives the body its necessary supply of Vitamin A and thirty grammes, Vitamin C.

21 Why were spices once so precious?

Pepper, ginger, cinnamon, mace and nutmeg, saffron, cumin, coriander, cassia and senna.

These are all spices once used far more than they are today to flavour and preserve food, as well as in medicines and cosmetics.

They were valued by the Europeans for their many uses. And because they came from Africa and Asia, their import into Europe involved long and difficult voyages.

So, cities in important positions along the route, such as Venice in Italy, became very rich.

It was the spice trade which made the Portuguese seek an eastern passage to India – and the Spanish to find another way, going west.

The first reached India.

The second ship, captained by the Italian Christopher Columbus, discovered America – but the fact that they were searching for a western route to India is borne out by the name Columbus gave to the land – the West Indies.

22 What is yoghurt?

Yoghurt is milk subjected to the action of a special fermentation which has the power to fight bacteria harmful to the intestine.

The shepherds of Eastern Europe and Asia knew of yoghurt in ancient times. It is even spoken of in the Bible – and in Asia Minor, it was used by the Bulgarians, the Romanians and the Turks.

As for nutritional value, yoghurt is equal to milk – but much lower in sugar.

23 Why is milk a complete food?

Milk is produced by all mammals to feed their young.

Women produce milk for their babies, cows produce milk for their calves, the mare for her foals, and so on.

In fact, the young of mammals are fed solely on milk from birth – human babies up to three or four months old. Young mammals continue to feed on milk, even when they are introduced to solid foods.

This shows that milk has everything we need – protein, fats, lactose and the minerals potassium, sodium, calcium, magnesium, iron and phosphorus.

Once cows have been milked, the milk is taken in a tanker to a collection centre, where it is first pasteurised – raised to a high temperature within a few seconds – so that germs are killed without the taste of milk being affected.

The second process is homogenisation – which, by breaking down the fat particles in the milk, makes it more digestible.

Then, the milk is ready to be kept for a while!

24 Which plants and animals came from America?

When European sailors came to America they were introduced to many new plants and animals, as well as habits and customs, and the native Americans were fascinated by the horses – an animal which had been extinct in their continent for thousands of years.

But by the end of the second voyage by Columbus, they knew about pigs – and in return they brought goats, hens and oxen, and crops such as corn, barley, rye and rice, citrus fruits and vines.

On their return to Europe, they unloaded potatoes, tomatoes, peppers, sunflowers, pineapples, prickly pears, courgettes and almost every type of bean, maize, sweet potatoes, ground nuts, tobacco and turkeys!

There were also cocoa and vanilla. And with America having shown itself as an ideal place for cultivation of sugar cane on a big scale, the use of sugar soon began to spread rapidly.

And so each civilisation enriched the lives of the other.

25 When was the fork invented?

Of all the cutlery that we use today, the first to appear was certainly the knife. Then there were spoons – first shells, then carved wood, then proper spoons with handles of wood or metal, and ladles, as well. Before any of this, people fed themselves with their hands.

The biggest change came about with the fork, which appeared in Italy in the 18th century and then spread to France and the United Kingdom.

26 Is there a bread tree?

The Bread Tree (*Artocarpus*) from Southern Asia, a relative of our own mulberry tree, produces fleshy fruit that is rich in starch, rather like bread.

Among other trees throughout the world which bear unusual fruits, there is the Venezuelan "milk tree" (*Galactodendron utile*) producing a sweet-tasting milk, not unlike ordinary milk, which can be obtained by tapping the trunk.

The African "butter tree" produces seeds which, when minced and boiled with water give a sort of butter – and people can obtain a type of butter or "mowrah" from a similar sort of tree in India.

In Peru there is the "tomato tree" (*Cyphomandra betacea*) with fruit similar to the tomato which can be eaten fresh or cooked to make a sort of jam or chutney.

Or, we could eat the fruit of the African "salami tree" (*Kigelia aethiopica*) which bears salami-like fruit, half a metre long and weighing up to six kilos!

27 When did the use of tea spread?

Tea was grown and drunk in China between 600 A.D. and 800 A.D. From there, it was drunk in Japan more than 1,000 years ago. In the 16th century, the Portuguese discovered it in China, but it was the Dutch who brought tea to Europe in the 17th century and by the beginning of the 18th century, tea had spread to England. It was the Europeans, too, who developed tea-growing in the colonies of Java, Ceylon (now Sri Lanka), India and Kenya.

28 What sort of food is an egg?

We know that all living things are made up of cells, usually visible only under the microscope.

But there is one cell big enough to be seen by the naked eye – the egg.

An egg contains all the nutrition which is required to feed and nourish a developing chick so that it will be strong and healthy.

But a chick will only be born if the egg produced by the hen is fertilised by the cockerel.

Otherwise, it can be eaten, both by animals and humans.

A hen's egg is rich in protein and fats, low in carbohydrate. It is also very rich in calcium.

Many animals raid the nests of birds and reptiles, such as turtles and crocodiles – which is why they keep watch over their nests, ready to defend their young.

This is why it is best not to disturb a hen when she is sitting on her eggs.

There are many ways of using eggs – raw, boiled, fried, poached, scrambled, coddled or baked, or as ingredients in cooking.

29 When was the cooking pot invented?

It was about 10,000 years ago that man began farming and breeding animals.

They also began to model clay which they baked in ovens to make containers for their produce, the results of all their hard work.

And so there came on the scene basins and pots both for cooking and eating the different types of food which they now ate.

For plates and dishes, people used shells and carved wood, with baskets and bags made of leather for hunting and gathering food and cups and jugs for drinking and milking cows.

Using cooking pots, they could make porridge and puddings from cereals, as well as cooking soup in a different way to the one described for 2nd October.

The first cooking pots were made with clay modelled by hand, or by coiling around a long sausage of clay.

But when the potter's wheel was invented, a potter could make quantities of containers of various sizes, decorating them more and more elaborately and with style and elegance.

30 How did the Ancient Romans eat?

To begin with, the Ancient Romans ate seated on the floor.

Then, as they became richer, they copied the more refined way of life of the Etruscans and the Greeks, building houses with dining rooms where they would eat lying down on beds.

Slaves would bring them dishes to choose from, then cut the food into pieces which they served on plates for the nobles to help themselves with their hands.

31 When did we first start eating potatoes?

There is a story of how the famous French agriculturalist, Antoine-Augustin Parmentier, tricked people into growing and eating potatoes.

He planted a field of potatoes and paid for soldiers to keep watch.

Then, he spread the rumour that the vegetable planted was destined only for the tables of the rich – relying on the curiosity both of the people and the soldiers.

As Parmentier guessed, this made everyone want to try potatoes. And when they discovered how good they were, they soon began to grow and to eat them!

This may only be a story. But it is a fact that in 1789, the year of the French Revolution, Parmentier wrote his "Paper on the Cultivation and Use of Potatoes".

Potatoes were grown in America from ancient times in great quantities. Some varieties adapted to the high altitude of the Andes Mountains, where, in 1538, a Spanish soldier discovered them by chance in a valley in Columbia.

Fifty years later, they were brought to Europe – although their importance in the European diet came a long while afterwards, thanks to Parmentier.

Now, Europe produces almost half the potatoes in the world.

The biggest growers, apart from Russia, are Poland and Germany. Poland alone produces more than three times the quantity of potatoes grown in South America, where they came from originally.

COMMUNICATIONS

The Key to a Mystery

The Key to a Mystery

IN A SCHOOL at Grenoble, in 1801, there was a boy who, despite poor exam results in his home town of Figeac, in Southern France, had shown a great flair for languages.

At only 11 years of age, Jean-Francois Champollion already had an exceptional knowledge of Latin and Greek and was studying Hebrew with great success – thanks to his elder brother, who, recognising the genius of Jean-Francois, had taken him to Grenoble. It was a lot different to Figeac, but the boy loved his new school.

Then one day the famous scientist Fourier came on a visit. He had followed Napoleon to Egypt and was very interested in the Ancient Egyptian civilisation.

And, as he spoke with the young Jean-Francois, he could not help being impressed by his lively mind and his intelligence.

When it was time for him to go, Fourier said, "I'd like to talk to you a little more. Can you come to my house? I have some interesting things I'd like you to see!"

Of course, Jean-Francois went along.

And at Fourier's house he saw things which few people in the whole of Europe had ever seen – treasures from Ancient Egypt!

He was fascinated by the papyruses covered with symbols and drawings – the same symbols and drawings which were carved on shiny slabs of stone, statues and a host of other objects.

"Those signs," said Jean-Francois at last, "what are they?"

"Hieroglyphics," Fourier told him. "The writings of Ancient Egypt!"

"Writings?" echoed the boy in wonder. "But what are they about?"

"I do not know," Fourier admitted. "Nobody has yet been able to find out what any of it means!"

"Is it so difficult?"

"Very difficult," nodded the scientist. "If we were lucky enough to find something written in a language which we know, as well as the hieroglyphics... then we would be able to understand."

"And did you search really hard?" asked the boy.

"Certainly!" Fourier smiled. "All Napoleon's soldiers and the French officials in Egypt had to show everything they found, no matter how unimportant it

seemed. And each time a crate arrived in Cairo, we always hoped there might be an inscription which would be the key to help us begin to understand this writing."

"But," Fourier continued, "finding such an inscription would be just the first step towards the solution of this great mystery!"

All this time, the man was watching Jean-Francois.

From the way he was looking at the Egyptian treasures, it was clear that he had something special – a hunger for knowledge, an insatiable curiosity, and a mind which worked at an astonishing speed.

"What are you thinking, Jean-Francois?" he asked at last.

The boy turned towards him, a serious expression on his face.

"When I am older," he said, speaking very slowly, "I shall read these inscriptions!"

Fourier laid a hand on the boy's shoulder.

"And I shall help you," he promised. "I will send copies of all the inscriptions which we get from Egypt. And if ever we find an inscription in two languages, you will be among the first to see it! I give you my word, Jean-Francois!"

Both of them kept to their part of the bargain.

Fourier sent Jean-Francois Champollion copies of all the Egyptian finds.

And, as Jean-Francois learned one language after another, so he studied the hieroglyphics of Ancient Egypt with an all consuming passion.

Then, one day there came to light a newly-found inscription. It was carved on a tablet of dark basalt rock, unearthed by a soldier at a place called Rosetta on the River Nile.

The inscription was in three languages – one of which was Greek!

They had found the key to unlock the mystery of the writings of the Pharoahs!

But, just as Fourier had said, the slab from Rosetta was only the first step.

For many years after, students from all over Europe came to see the famous "Rosetta Stone" and to study the writings of Ancient Egypt.

But it was Jean-Francois Champollion who found the first key to begin unravelling the mystery in 1821!

The boy had kept his promise.

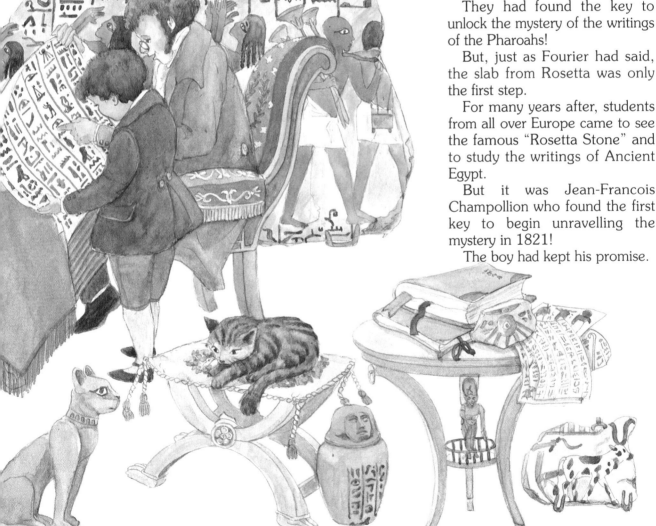

1 Where do we get the word "bible" from?

The word "bible" comes from the Greek and means "a collection of books". It is based on the word "biblion" meaning from the city of Biblo, now Jubayl in Lebanon, not far from Beirut. It was from Biblo that the Egyptian civilisation spread into Syria around 5000 years ago. So, it was an important trade centre for papyrus. And as they wrote on papyruses, the Greeks called them "biblos" meaning the papyrus from Biblo.

2 Is paper an ancient product?

A Roman historian was once asked by a student, "which product today would most help an Ancient Roman?" The answer was – paper.

With so much paper in use today, it is hard to believe that it was virtually unknown to ordinary people until a few centuries ago.

Although paper was made in China in 200 B.C. it was 800 A.D. before its use began extending to the Eastern world. Then, towards 1150 A.D. the Arabs brought it to Spain, and from there it spread throughout Europe. For around 500 years, it was made by hand using pieces of hemp, linen, cotton, jute, wood, straw, bamboo, broom, reeds and waste paper. Only towards the end of the 18th century did industrial paper-making begin, which led to much more paper being used and bought at affordable prices.

Before that, people used rolls of papyrus, animal skins, waxed tablets of wood, earthenware, fabric – almost anything which would stand writing or carving.

3 What were the first writings?

The oldest example of writing appeared in Mesopotamia more than 6000 years ago. It is called Cuneiform Writing, done by pressing a stick carved into triangular sections on to bars of fresh clay, making wedge-shaped characters which formed words and sentences. Then the bar would be left to dry.

Later on, the Ancient Egyptians wrote all their hieroglyphics on papyrus with coloured inks.

4 How do bees communicate with each other?

Honey-bees live in quite complex communities.

They also have an elaborate "class structure" in which each individual knows its place, doing its job to help the the community run smoothly.

The hive of honey-bees is always a busy place! But it is always quite orderly, with each bee knowing exactly what it has to do.

But, that is not all. Honey-bees also possess an extraordinary sense of direction, and can send messages to each other – by dancing....

So, what it is that honey-bees "say"? And how do they "talk"?

Well, they fly all day long in search of flowers from which they can take nectar back to the hive, ready to be made into honey.

When a bee finds a place with plenty of flowers from which it can get lots of nectar, it flies to honey-bees nearby to tell them.

Then each one does a circular dance in the air, to tell other bees that they have found flowers some distance from the hive!

5 Is there a "language of flowers"?

Everyone knows that the rose is a symbol of love and affection, and orange blossom is lucky for a bride.

But not so long ago, flowers were widely used to send special messages.

A girl would be hurt to receive a bunch of hydrangea, because it meant someone thought she was a boaster. But a pansy enclosed with a letter was the sign that the writer was thinking of that person; and the marigold, a sign of jealousy!

Ivy meant eternal loyalty, whilst the cornflower said, "I love you. But I am rather shy."

A student would thank a friend for help by sending a dahlia. A bunch of asters sent before an examination would say, "I have faith in you". And for a promotion or a sporting triumph, camellias, carnations or hyacinths might be sent.

And for some comfort after defeat?

A bunch of harebells ("Success crown your wishes"), or Marguerites "I respect you".

6 How did crowns and crowning begin?

In ancient times, a crown was woven from branches as a special type of headgear to put on holy statues as a sign of homage.

Gradually, they were made for monarchs and priests, as a sign of royal as well as sacred authority, plus those God had blessed with sporting triumphs, artistic achievement or victory in battle. Crowns were made of different materials, but generally gold and precious jewels, whilst a prize-winning poet would receive a crown of laurel.

Egyptian Pharoahs wore a double crown, symbolising the union of Higher and Lower Egypt, and in Greece and Rome they made crowns from flowers and greenery.

From the 17th century, crowns were for the nobility, too – people such as princes and princesses, dukes and duchesses, lords and ladies, counts, countesses and baronets.

Famous crowns include the iron crown for St. Stephen, King of Poland 1001 – 1038, the crown for the Holy Roman Emperor Charlemagne, and Queen Victoria's crown.

7 Why do we give orange blossom to a bride?

In the Middle Ages, kings and princes, knights and jesters, lords and commoners went to free the Holy Land from invasion. They had a cross embroidered on their tunics and called themselves "Crusaders", convinced that they would find savages in the East. Instead, they came back dazzled by all they had seen.

At that time, even kings in Europe had harsh lives. Castles inside were often as cold as the fields outside. Glass was rare and so windows had to be narrow and high. There was little furniture, fabrics were rough, food was simple and beds simply mattresses of straw.

Those first Crusaders did not expect to see lovely, airy houses, beautifully furnished with soft beds and people wearing clothes of silk and damask.

So, when they came back home they brought lots of things back with them – including the custom of a husband giving his bride on their wedding day a bunch of orange blossom, symbol of fruitfulness.

8 How do dogs communicate?

Howls, growls, snarls, barks... all these make up the language each dog can understand, together with the movement of the tail, the ears, the head and the way it walks.

But a dog also communicates when it is out by a look or sound or by leaving its own particular smell.

Then each dog passing will sniff and get the message – "This is where I have been, and this is my patch!"

9 How many different calendars are there?

From ancient times, men have divided time and regulated their work according to the different phases of the moon, the four seasons of the year, and the annual cycle of the stars.

A calendar is a way of setting this down; the one used mostly is the Gregorian calendar, which came into being in 1582.

A calendar also sets down religious holidays – so, in many countries, a traditional religious calendar is used as well. Israel has an ancient lunar-solar calendar with months alternating between 30 and 29 days, like Muslim countries, where years are counted from 16th July 622, the date of Mohammed's flight from Mecca to Medina.

In some Muslim countries, the Gregorian calendar has replaced the traditional one; in others the two are used, and in others the Gregorian calendar is not used.

In Japan, the years are counted from 660 B.C. when the legendary emperor, Jimmu-Tenno was crowned.

10 What are the Greek and Cyrillic alphabets?

The Greeks based their letters on the Phoenician alphabet, gradually altering them and changing the direction – Phoenicians writing from right to left, Greeks writing from left to right.

The Cyrillic alphabet was based on the Greek capital letters and taught by St. Cyril – hence its name – a Greek missionary of the 9th century who went to convert the Slavonic people, despite the teachings of their German rulers.

11 How did our alphabet begin?

Our alphabet originated from the Phoenician. Whilst the Greeks altered the Phoenician letters as they wanted, in Italy the Etruscans did the same, but keeping the Phoenician direction of writing from right to left.

The Romans adapted the Etruscan alphabet, changing the form of the letters but not the direction. The Roman alphabet then spread throughout their empire, alongside that of the Greek.

12 What were the schools like in Ancient Greece?

Schools were private in Ancient Greece, but they were controlled by the state and sometimes by the rulers.

A school did not need any title or special building – just an educated person to become the teacher and take lessons wherever he chose.

There were courses of study for boys from 7 to 18 years of age where they could learn grammar, mathematics, music, physical education, and other subjects.

Then – usually once a course had been completed – boys could go on to study under one of the great masters.

With the hot climate of Greece, many of these masters gave lessons in the open air.

Pupils were glad of the porches, the porticos and covered arcades, where they could walk just as the great philosopher Aristotle liked to do, or sit in the shade.

"Ordinary" schooling would have been like our secondary schools.

Advanced study can be compared to university education today.

13 What were the schools like in Ancient Rome?

The Romans wanted schools for their sons before anything else. Then, when Rome conquered Greece, many educated Greeks came to Rome to be teachers – and it was fashionable to go to Greece to study. Around 100 B.C. the state set up some schools, although tutors were still free to open private schools. Discipline was the same in all schools in Ancient Rome, with corporal punishment and the absence of summer holidays.

14 What about schools in the Middle Ages?

With the fall of the Roman Empire, Europe was invaded by people who had little time for culture and learning. So all over the continent, a network was set up through monasteries and churches, to establish centres where the Christian faith and its culture could be preserved – and so the only schools in the Middle Ages were those which existed to preserve and spread the religion – and which, from the 8th century, had to be run without charge. Then in the 9th century, the Holy Roman Emperor Charlemagne and other major sovereigns began promoting culture.

Their efforts were rewarded when, in 1000 A.D. the "Middle Classes" began to develop – people who wanted schools which were not centred solely on religion and who decided to set up their own.

These communal schools prepared students for work, and in addition to Latin, the "official" European language, they learned their own "local" languages too.

15 When did universities begin?

The university system was the way in which the Middle Classes firmly established themselves. For around five hundred years, schools had remained in the hands of the churches, providing only teachers of religion and neglecting other areas of learning. The Middle Classes wanted to learn about those subjects which had been neglected, to help them in their trading and to draw up rules and regulations for their successors.

They needed to know mathematics, medicine, natural science and astronomy. And so, they set up associations or "universities" of students and masters. And, as in Ancient Greece, these schools of higher education did not have to follow any orders of the state. However, differences sometimes arose between students or professors, or within the city where it was founded, and so the university moved on, either wholly or in part.

One famous example is Oxford University, founded by rebels from the University of Paris.

16 What is the Linnaeus Classification?

Carl von Linne was a Swedish boy who went into the country as often as he could, collecting herbs and flowers. In the end, his teachers despaired, and his parents sent him to be an apprentice shoe-maker. But a doctor, seeing how gifted the boy really was, gave him scientific books to read, then persuaded his father to allow him to study. Carl took his degree at Uppsala and in 1735, at only 28 years old, he published a 12-page booklet entitled *"Systema naturae"* – the System of Nature – which dealt with animals, and *"Species plantarum"* – Species of Plants - listing all living things in the easiest way ever known. Each animal or plant on these lists was identified by a name, indicating the type and an adjective to indicate the species, and written in Latin, so as to be understood by all scientists.

Thanks to him, Germans know that *Urtica dioica* means *"Brennessel"*, Italians *"ortica"* – and in English? A stinging nettle!

17 What is the story behind the laurel wreath?

Daphne was a most beautiful nymph, daughter of the god of the River Pinios, who lived in the Thessaly region of Greece.

In fact, Daphne was so beautiful that the god Apollo fell in love with her. And although Daphne always rejected Apollo's love, he refused to be beaten.

One day, as Daphne fled, Apollo chased her. She was quick, but he was much faster. In desperation, Daphne prayed to the great goddess Thea, who, not really thinking about what she did, changed Daphne into a laurel – which is what "Daphne" means in Greek.

From then on, the laurel became the plant sacred to Apollo. And because Apollo was the god of the arts, it became a symbol of knowledge, success and fame – with a crown of laurel being given to poets, sporting champions and all those who excell and triumph in some field.

This tradition continues today, with a laurel wreath still given to Britain's Poet Laureate and professors of leading universities.

18 How did printing and movable type begin?

It was in the middle of the 15th century that the German Johann Gutenberg invented printing with movable type – assembling wooden letters of the alphabet to set out text for the pages of a book in a frame. The text was inked, then put face down on to paper beneath a press.

Copies of a book could be printed this way, instead of being written by hand as they were before, and available to only a very few people.

19 What is the "mass media"?

Media is a term for methods of communication – radio, television, newspapers, magazines, leaflets, books, videos, tapes, etc. Of these, radio, television and newspapers affect so many different types of people, they are defined as "mass media" – methods of communication for the masses.

The mass media influences fashion, products, life-styles – even standards of living – in the way they inform, promote goods and influence public opinion. The number of T.V. sets, radios and amount of published material is an indication of a country's wealth. For example, in Asia – Japan, a country of 123,000,000 people, has over 100,000,000 radios and 80,000,000 televisions; India, a country of 700,000,000 people, has 65,000,000 radios and 6,000,000 televisions. In Africa, Kenya, with 20,000,000 people, has 2,000,000 radios and 100,000 television s. Sudan's 21,000,000 people have 6,000,000 radios and just over 1,000,000 television sets. 26,000,000 people in Canada have 29,000,000 radios and 16,000,000 television sets; in Columbia, South America, 28,000,000 people have 8,000,000 radios and 5,500,000 T.V. sets.

In Europe, Sweden's 8,500,000 people have 7,500,000 radios and 3,500,000 T.V. sets; 10,000,000 people in Greece have 4,000,000 radios and 2,000,000 T.V. sets. And, to finish, Australia – 16,500,000 people with 30,000,000 radios and 5,000,0000 T.V. sets.

20 What is the International Alphabet?

The International Alphabet is a way of communicating by radio, used by pilots, radio operators, and so on. It makes dialogue possible between people who speak different languages or when words are distorted by either pronunciation or faulty transmission.

In the International Alphabet, each letter is replaced by a word beginning with that letter – so YORK would be communicated as Yankee, Oscar, Romeo, Kilo.

21 How do ships communicate?

Ever since the early days of sail, men have had ways of communicating with other ships and with the land. Sailors worldwide understand the language of flags.

A flag at half mast means mourning; a square yellow flag means a ship is in quarantine; a ship at war flying a white flag shows that they mean to do battle – whilst to lower the white flag means that the ship wants to surrender.

A "courtesy flag" is that of a foreign state and which is hoisted by ships entering a port belonging to that state.

Of these courtesy flags, a square white flag means "do not disturb"; a square, blue flag with a diagonal white line means that the host is on board; a square blue flag with the white outline of a glass at its centre is an invitation to come on board.

Using the internationally-known Semaphore System, a person holds two flags in special ways to spell out the letters of the alphabet.

A ._	H	O ___	V ..._	Y _.__
B _...	I ..	P ._ _.	W ._ _	Z _ _..
C _._.	J ._ _ _	Q _ _._	X _.._	
D _..	K _._	R ._.		
E .	L ._..	S ...		
F .._.	M _ _	T _		
G _ _.	N _.	U .._		

22 What is the Morse Code?

The Morse Code came to be used with the telegraph, with dots and dashes representing letters.

The operator presses the morse tapper more or less than a second to send a short dot, or a long dash. The message is sent from the tapper to a receiver and activates a pointed lever which writes on a strip of paper the sequence of dots and dashes. Then the telegraphist reads the strip and deciphers the message.

23 What is Esperanto?

Esperanto is the most widely used artificial, international language. By "artificial", we mean a language which has not developed naturally, but has been defined within certain rules and aims. The main aim of Esperanto is that it should be understood worldwide.

It was invented by a Polish doctor called Zamenhof, who demonstrated it in his work *Linguo Internacia* in 1887. He gave himself the name *Doktor Esperanto* meaning "Doctor Hopeful" in his new language, so "Esperanto" became the name of the language.

Esperanto has spread throughout the world, with its own magazines, translations, radio programmes and conferences, thanks to its easy grammar and phonetic simplicity, with every letter corresponding to its actual sound.

The basic vocabulary consists of words founded on the Germanic and Slavonic languages, but mainly the Romance languages – Italian, Portuguese, Spanish, French and Rumanian.

24 How many languages are spoken throughout the world?

Within each main language of the world, there are many local and regional variations, called dialects. Names by which things are called, pronunciation, the use of verbs, structure of sentences – all these can vary a great deal from one locality to another.

For instance, there is the French spoken in Brittany, the French spoken in Provence, the French spoken in Alsace, etc.

So, how many languages are spoken throughout the world? National and local languages and dialects make up hundreds of thousands – nobody can say exactly how many.

But looking at languages spoken by a considerable number of people, we can say that there must be around 3,500 languages spoken worldwide.

We can get some idea of the difficulty in arriving at a more precise number when we consider that there are 700 translations of the Bible – and 700 is the very minimum number of languages spoken and written through the world.

25 Who invented the telegraph and the telephone?

Samuel Morse received a laurel wreath at Yale University, U.S.A. at only eighteen years old, before going to England to study painting.

Returning to America, he became an apprentice portrait painter – but in 1835, he introduced the first electric telegraph machine. The money to set up a telegraph system was granted eight years later, and in 1844, the first message was sent from Washington to Baltimore. Soon, telegraph poles and wires became part of the scenery.

Italian-born Antonio Meucci emigrated to Havana at the age of twenty-five, becoming a theatre mechanic before going to the U.S.A. where he opened a candle factory. He had the idea of a telephone in Havana, and although he could not finance this, he took out a patent for two years on his invention.

So when Bell and Grey sought a patent for their telephone, Meucci took legal action. The court ruled that the invention of the telephone was his – but, alas, he could not develop it.

26 When was the radio invented?

"Go behind the hill, and if you hear a signal, fire a shot!" said young Guglielmo Marconi to one of the men employed by his father. It was 1895, and they were used to the boy working with electric cables and putting strange devices on the roof. So, the man just went behind the hill – and when he heard the signal, gave a shot.

Guglielmo Marconi had done it! In 1896, he applied for a patent "for a communication system by means of electro-magnetic waves" – radio. Marconi offered the Italian government the rights to his invention; when they refused, he went to England to continue his research.

In 1901, the first message was sent between Cornwall and America. A Europe-America radio-telegraph service beginning a year later. In 1909, radio saved 2000 passengers on the English steamship *Republic* and many governments made radio compulsory on ships. And in 1920 the B.B.C. began the first regular radio programme service.

27 When was the television invented?

The "grandfather" of television was Polish-born Paul Nipkow. He built a machine in the form of a disc which "broke up" images into dots and transmitted them. The "father" of television was the Scot, John Logie Baird. His "telecamera" transmitted images into the next room in 1925. In 1935, the first T.V. transmissions began in New York, followed by Berlin and London. In 1953, the first colour television appeared in the U.S.A.

28 What is a "status symbol"?

By the word "status", we mean a particular placing in a social structure – the status of a city dweller, the head of a family and so on.

From ancient times, the status of a person was seen by various exterior signs – such as Coats of Arms for the nobility, clergymen's vestments, the feathered head-dresses of American red Indians, the red spot in the centre of foreheads of high caste Indian people, magistrates' robes, the uniforms of military services and mortarboards worn by University professors.

There are also modern status symbols, arising from the consumer society in which we live – fast cars, designer clothes, expensive watches, car telephones...

Many may be passing fancies – styles in clothes, things which are fashionable for a time, then go out of date – the ponytail, the mini-skirt, the Swatch watch.

So, a status symbol is something which the mass media persuades us that we must have, in order to be considered smart, up-to-date and successful.

But there is an ever-present danger of people buying things they do not really need.

What use is an expensive car which can cruise at 100 m.p.h. if there are speed limits in force?

And people become champion skiers and titles-holders in tennis through sheer hard work and hours of practice – not "famous name" rackets or designer sports clothes .

29 What is the significance of the caduceus?

The ancient sign of the caduceus can still be seen outside some old-established chemists and pharmacies. To the Ancient Greeks, this wand with two serpents coiled around it, represented the balance between good and bad – the venom of the snake which can kill and the venom which can cure. The caduceus was carried by the messenger-god Hermes, and was also the sign of Asclepius, Greek god of medicine.

30 What is etiquette?

In 1558, an Italian by the name of Giovani della Casa wrote a book called "Etiquette Rather Than Habit".

The theme had been suggested to him by Galeazzo Florimonte, a bishop, and the work soon became famous.

In it, the writer gave advice to a young man on the correct way to speak, to dress, to behave at table and to treat people, listing everything which should be avoided.

The book set out all the rules to follow and by which a person is judged to be well mannered.

And although the incorrect use of cutlery or drinking glasses at the dining table today is easily forgiven, it is still a sign of bad manners or lack of etiquette.

For instance – what about people who telephone without saying their name properly?

People who butt into conversations? Who shout in public places, and who do not treat old people with respect? Who refuse to remain in a queue?

People who borrow things and return them damaged, or don't return them at all?

People who disturb lessons at school? Who leave litter? Who have their radios on too loud? Who sound their car horns when it is not necessary?

With bigger populations, examples of bad manners are more numerous than at the time of Giovanni della Casa.

If he were alive today, he would need to write a much longer book in order to cover every possible example and teach people how to correct and improve their etiquette!

PLANTS AND ANIMALS

The Story of Ram

The Story of Ram

IN THE FERTILE PLAINS and forests of Central Europe, there once lived a proud race of people who farmed the land, bred cattle and worked with metal.

These were the Celts and they had their own priests, called druids, who were very knowledgeable and wise, making herbal medicines and able to interpret the signs of nature.

All village chiefs listened to the druids with great respect, asking their advice both in peace and war, whilst ordinary people went to them with their problems.

Every so often, the druids had meetings, where they would gather together in a forest, exchanging news and advice and learning new things to help their villages.

One old druid who was going had an apprentice, a boy called Ram.

"I shall return at the next full moon," he told Ram. "By now, you can take my place in many ways, and the people are at peace, the harvest promises to be good and the cattle are calm and quiet. Guide them with your wisdom and always look towards nature as your most powerful master."

Ram was kept very busy.

He prepared a medicine for the village chief to ease him stomach, and for his son who had been injured whilst on a hunt. He talked with a woman who had been having bad dreams, and chose the finest animals to decorate for the animal festival which would be held to celebrate the return of the old druid.

Next day, Ram was in his hut in the middle of the forest when there came a boy from the village.

"Come quickly, Druid!" he cried. "Three men have fallen to the ground, hot with fever! A woman is screaming because of a pain all over her body! And a baby has blue marks on its face!"

Ram wasted no time. Seizing the bag containing medical potions, he ran after the boy.

But by the time he arrived at the village, the fever had already spread.

Many more people were in great pain and some had blue marks on their faces. Ram had never seen such marks – and he could find no signs as to what was causing the pain.

Before very long, the first man who had fallen ill died. In desperation, Ram tried medicines

and potions to fight the mysterious fever, but nothing seemed to be any good.

Had the people eaten poisonous food? Had they been bitten or stung?

Then another man died. More deaths followed. It was a plague, an unknown disease against which Ram was powerless.

After three days, the young Druid could only cry with those who were suffering. The disease appeared merciless and their busy, happy village had become a sad place where people were living in fear.

Ram returned to his hut, hoping to find medicines which he had not yet tried. But there was nothing.

In despair, he went to a sacred oak tree in the forest.

Beneath the tree, he begged and prayed for his people, almost beside himself with grief and so weary that, in the end, he fell asleep.

As he slept, there appeared a majestic-looking man, holding a stick, with a snake coiled around it.

The man used this stick to show Ram a branch of mistletoe, telling him how to extract a medicine from it. Then the man disappeared – and Ram awoke.

Rubbing his eyes, he found himself looking up into the branches of the oak tree – and it was then that he saw the mistletoe.

Beginning to feel more hopeful, he picked some and prepared the medicine, doing just as the man in his dream had said.

Then he ran to the village and gave the potion to the sick people.

That night, there was no weeping or cries of pain. For the first time in many weeks, the sick slept peacefully.

And the day after, it was clear that Ram's potion had conquered the plague.

The people wept with joy and blessed the young druid, knowing that, very slowly, life would return to normal.

From then on, the mistletoe was looked upon as a sacred plant. And on the last night of each year, people hung mistletoe on their door, leaving it there until the first morning of the New Year to protect their home from illness.

It is a custom which many people in Europe carry out to this day – and all thanks to a young druid called Ram.

1 How do flowers attract insects?

The brilliant papery petals of the poppies and the sunflowers. The unusual beauty of the snapdragon. The heady perfume of the jasmine. None of these are given by nature for the pleasure of human beings. Instead, these are the methods by which flowers attract insects.

Bees, flies, butterflies.... as they fly from flower to flower sucking the delicious nectar, so they carry the pollen by which a flower can reproduce.

2 Why are insects important to plants?

As we saw on the 1st December, plants produce flowers which attract insects. Landing on the flowers to suck the nectar, the insects become covered with pollen, a fine powder produced by the male organs of a plant.

And when they go on to another flower, the pollen is deposited on the female organs, fertilising them and so beginning a new plant.

Not all plants need insects so that they can reproduce – but those which do have many different ways of attracting them.

Those attracting bees have yellow and blue flowers, because bees do not see the colour red. Those visited by night butterflies have white, highly perfumed flowers which open only at night.

Plants have spent one hundred and fifty million years adapting themselves to the world in which we live. So, when man alters the natural balance and destroys a type of insect, plants depending on these insects for their reproduction also disappear.

3 What are fungi?

By "fungi", botanists can mean an enormous number of living things – from the common mildew to the finest mushroom – vegetable matter which has no green chlorophyll. So, because they are unable to produce for themselves the nutriments which they need, they take these from other plant life. There are many types of fungi, some good to eat and some poisonous. Only the experts know how to tell for certain those which are harmless.

4 What is a Phoenix?

According to legend, the phoenix was a bird rather like a huge eagle with brightly coloured feathers. It came from Ethiopia and lived on average for 500 years, fed on pearls and incense.

When it was near to death, the phoenix was said to build itself a nest of sweet-smelling herbs and lay down, ready to die in the flames – and from the ashes of the nest there arose another phoenix.

This mythical bird was sacred to the Egyptians and became a symbol of resurrection for Christians.

It was soon discovered that the phoenix never existed – and the saying, "the bird everyone talks about but nobody knows," was popular right up until the 18th century.

Because of the characteristics of the phoenix, the name also came to mean a person or a thing which is rare, or never found. "Your intelligence is like a phoenix!" was an insult. "You are a phoenix among friends!" was a compliment.

5 Why do plants turn towards the light?

Light is essential to green plants. It activates the green chlorophyll, giving it energy for the process of photosynthesis, necessary for the life of the plant.

Each plant needs a certain amount of light.

The violet likes the shade, tropical plants need the sun, and the mallow adapts to any amount of light.

So, before deciding the position of a plant, we need to know what it needs.

A violet in full sun will wither, whereas the growth of any tropical plant in the shade will be stunted.

Direction is also important. Plants which strain towards the light, or with long stems and small leaves are not getting enough light. Plants with stems which are too weak for their leaves have too much light.

With potted plants, pots must be turned round so that each part of the plant gets enough light.

But whenever a plant is transplanted into a more suitable place – just see how it grows!

6 When did dinosaurs live?

Dinosaurs lived in the Mesozoic Age, lasting from 225 million to 65 million years ago.

During this time there grew huge conifer and palm trees, ferns, flowering plants and tall grasses.

In the sea there lived fish, algae, coral, jellyfish, sponges, and a little later, molluscs – snails, limpets, cuttlefish, etc. and sea urchins.

On Earth there were hundreds of insects, amphibians and reptiles, followed by primitive mammals, some of which still survive – the Duck-billed Platypus, Spiny Echidna, and marsupials with their babies in a pouch – all from Australia.

The dinosaurs ranged from the Deinonychus at 2.5 metres long, to the Apatosaurus – otherwise known as the Brontosaurus – at 20 metres, and the Iguanadon at 40 metres.

Some ate plants, some were meat-eaters. And because of their enormous size, many needed vast amounts of food.

But they did not attack man – because man was not yet on earth. The first human beings came into existence about 3 million years ago – whereas dinosaurs existed only up until 65 million years ago when mysteriously they all died out.

We know about the structure of the bones and muscles of many dinosaurs from the fossilised skeletons which have been excavated. But we know little about their skins.

It was once thought that all dinosaurs had scaly bodies – but recent studies have shown that some were hairy.

7 Which plants are said to be "officinal"?

"Officinal" comes from the Latin "officinalis", meaning "workshop", which chemists in ancient times used to call the places where they worked. So now, "officinal" plants are those which contain useful substances to help our bodies.

Digitalis, a drug which helps people with heart problems, comes from the foxglove. And for thousands of years, people have drunk camomile tea as an aid to restful sleep.

8 What animals and plants are there at the Poles?

The harsh climate at the North and South Poles may not seem encouraging to life.

There may be no lush plant-life in the Arctic, but there are mosses, lichens, various weeds and heathers.

Animals have adapted to the extreme cold with fur, layers of fat – and the camouflage colouring of white bears, seals, walruses, whales, the white musk ox, wolves, reindeer, various rodents and the husky dog. There are also numerous sea birds who migrate each year – and mosquitoes during the short Arctic summer!

South at the Antarctic, there is little vegetation, with hardly any moss or lichens and few insects, because life on the ground is reduced. But sea-life is far richer than at the North Pole, with penguins, migratory birds, four different types of seal, and whales.

And, man? In the Arctic there live the eskimos; and in the Antarctic, scientists from all over the world, because it is an ideal place for research.

9 What is camouflage?

A skier wanting to move unseen, would wear white clothes for camouflage – that is, imitating the colours of the surroundings, in the way that many plants and animals do – except that nature has given plants and animals ways of camouflage which no man could possibly equal!

For instance – at the poles, there live creatures with white fur or feathers; in the deserts, those with skins or feathers the colour of sand.

There are creatures who can adapt their colouring; insects with colouring similar to leaves, twigs, tree bark and stone; fish coloured blue on the back and white on the underside, so as not to be seen above or below; crustaceans which let little plants and animals grow on their shells so that they look like bits of the sea bed, whilst the sole can look like a plain piece of rock in the sea – the examples can go on for ever.

Camouflage is a means of defence, as well as a way for animals to catch their prey without being easily seen.

10 What are mosses and lichens?

Plants began life in water – primitive algae which adapted to watery surroundings and minimum warmth. On land there appeared fungi, then lichen, a form of symbiosis (see 19 December) between algae and fungi, and moss, a plant with little leaves, roots and stems, like bigger plants. Moss and lichen spread in almost every part of the Earth, from the Poles to the deserts, and in places where it seems that nothing could live.

11 What animals and plants are there in the desert?

Desert regions have very low rainfall, which means plant-life lasts only a short while. But as well as the sand, the desert has stony ground and rocky formations.

The temperature is remarkable, too, going from 50°C in the shade by day to minus 10°C at night. So the plants and animals who live there have had to adapt to the harsh conditions.

In the Sahara Desert, for example, plants have a very rapid cycle, flowering and reproducing during the short and rare rainy season, and their seeds surviving in the soil until the next rain, sometimes years ahead.

Perennial ("everlasting") plants have long roots to push them up in search of warmth, reduced leaves and bodies with reserves of water.

The animals which have adapted best are the reptiles and insects.

There are also various rodents, dromedaries and camels, antelopes, gazelles, goats, wolves and numerous birds.

12 Why are there oases in the desert?

An oasis springs up in the desert wherever there is a reserve of water, either on the surface or beneath the ground.

It was not nature who made them as luxurious as we see them in pictures, but men who dug holes and irrigated the water, planted date palms and tamarind trees, as well as tomato plants, onions, melons, courgettes and peppers, creating a little paradise in the middle of very hostile surroundings.

13 Which animals are not afraid of snakes?

In the regions where there are poisonous snakes, people still sleep soundly, protected by brave and clever animals!

The choice is between turkeys, pigs, hedgehogs and the mongoose – all enemies of the snake and unaffected by their poison.

Turkeys and pigs are set free to roam around, but they need looking after. But hedgehogs and the mongoose are very glad of a snake, as a change from a diet of insects!

14 What is moulting?

Many animals regularly renew their fur or feathers. This is moulting and can happen in many ways, according to the type of animals.

There are insects, and crustaceans with their bodies protected by a hard shell.

When it needs more space, the shell breaks, leaving the animal with a soft shell so that it can continue to grow. This new shell will harden in a matter of hours, and when the animal needs still more space, then this shell, too, will break.

Snakes and lizards moult each year in a similar way, casting aside their old skins.

Mammals do not moult. Dead cells of skins flake off continuously, and fur is also continually being renewed – although furry mammals grow thicker coats for winter, with some, such as ermine, changing colour for camouflage.

Birds moult feathers. With hens, this happens in autumn, and when they are not laying so many eggs.

15 Are gorillas dangerous?

The gorilla lives in Central Africa. Its front limbs are longer than the rear, and it has a broad chest, with flexible thumbs and big toes on its hands and feet. It is covered in thick black fur, except for its face.

It has canine teeth, grows up to 2 metres high and weighs up to 275 kilogrammes.

It is very strong – but it is a vegetarian and is not fierce. In fact, people have lived safely with gorillas for some time.

16 Which birds live in our cities?

We need not go far to see birds, even in cities. In fact, certain parts of a city are ideal for some birds. There is plenty of food, shelter from the cold, places where they can drink, and few enemies to worry them. It is calculated that in the city there can be as many birds as in a sizeable wood, and far more than in the open countryside.

Pigeons are the most common birds in a city. They have been tame for six thousand years and know very well how to live with people!

But the best "city-dwellers" are sparrows – far more numerous in the city than in the countryside. They are lively and sociable, although not as tame as pigeons.

The exception is the London sparrow, who often eats from the hands of Londoners.

In most cities, there are usually a number of swifts. These birds are champion fliers even when they are sleeping or mating in flight, or flying down in search of insects.

In parks and gardens we see blue-tits and great-tits on the look-out for nuts!

Blue-tits in Great Britain often peck milk-bottle tops on door-steps to take the cream from underneath!

In the city, we also see and hear blackbirds, chaffinches, robins, greenfinches, and seagulls.

And we must not forget the birds of prey, such as the owl.

In many cities throughout the world, storks and swallows return from spending the winter in Africa year after year to build their nests in the same places.

17 Do plants have feelings?

In an experiment, an electrode connected to a pen was clipped to a plant, then somebody went near that plant with a cigarette. The pen registered a surge equal to a cry of terror.

So, plants do have feelings – feelings of hunger and thirst, of joy, fear and love, wanting understanding and sympathy. Experiments also show that they like classical music – asters and petunias bloom to the sound of violins!

18 Where are the biggest trees in the world?

The highest are the eucalyptus trees; and the broadest around the trunk are the baobab trees in Africa and the sequoia trees in North America.

South east of San Francisco, is Sacramento, with its two National Parks – Kings Canyon and Sequoia. Here, these magnificent giants are planted and protected. Some of the sequoia trees are believed to be 2,000 to 2,500 years old; one could be up to 4,000 years old.

To know for sure, we would have to cut down the tree and count the rings! But who would cut down the "General Sherman", 90 metres high and with one branch 40 metres up from the ground more than 2 metres in diameter? Or the "General Grant", a memorial to all those who have fallen in'war? Or the "General Lee" named after the famous Confederate General?

With a diameter of 9.2 metres at the base, one "slice" from the "General Sherman" would have a surface of 67square metres – the area of a good-sized apartment!

19 What is symbiosis?

By symbiosis, we mean the joint life between two or more animals or plants.

The term was first used around 100 years ago for lichens, when it was was discovered that these were the result of an association between fungi and algae (see 10 December).

In true symbiosis, living things called parasites thrive on other living things – bacteria which live in the intestine and aid digestion; some fungi such as mushrooms and toadstools live in symbiosis with the roots of plants; many algae with some animals.

It seems, too, that the luminescence or glow of certain living things also applies to the things which live with them in symbiosis.

Symbiosis is also seen when the hermit crab, a crustacean with a soft stomach, goes into the empty shell of a sea snail to protect itself.

It is quite a sight to see a "sea snail" scuttling along with the tufts of the hermit crab sticking out!

20 Why do nettles sting?

Nettles sting because both the leaves and stem are covered with a skin which has cells containing little parcels of liquid. The slightest pressure breaks the fragile walls of the cells and releases the liquid – which irritates because it contains a high quantity of formic acid.

As it withers, the nettle loses its sting. Some people wear gloves to pick them, and, as they die off, use them in soups, salads and wines.

21 What is the "Victoria Regia"?

On 8th November 1849, Britain's Queen Victoria was presented with a most stupendous flower, named in her honour.

This was the "Victoria Regia", the biggest-ever water plant in the world.

It was discovered in the Amazon by a German botanist in 1801, and in 1846, was successfully grown in England – thanks to the gardeners at Chatsworth House, Bakewell in Derbyshire, who built a special greenhouse with a tank.

The leaves of the plant grew to six or seven metres in diameter, with the edge raised by 20 centimetres. And this enormous plant floated because of veins full of air which criss-crossed the interior.

The "Victoria Regia" could carry enormous weights, even a man! Its flowers were highly perfumed, with a diameter of 30 – 50 centimetres.

These opened at night, but for two nights only, changing colour from white the first night to pink or red the second night.

22 In what ways can we use the date palm trees?

An Arabian proverb says "even a camel grows dates at an oasis."

As well as eating the dates from palm trees, the leaves are used to make rush matting, ropes and roofing materials.

Burning the stem produces a sugary liquid to make into delicious non-alcoholic wine! Babylonians made vinegar, a type of honey and flour, too.

No wonder that, from ancient times, the palm has been called "The Tree of Life".

23 Where does the "Travellers' Tree" grow?

When European explorers found plants which they did not know, they would always bring back samples for study.

The film "Mutiny on the Bounty" is the true story of a voyage in search of exotic plants. But the water needed by the plants carried on the ship reduced water rations for the crew to such an extent that there was a revolt.

Many species were introduced to Europe.

One was an enormous tree from Madagascar, with leaves up to four metres long, similar to that of a banana, but spread out in a fan, and producing sprays of white flowers up to twelve metres in height.

At the base of their long stems, the leaves collected water, which would spurt out when the leaf was pierced at this spot.

Because of this, the tree was called "The Traveller's Tree".

But it is unlikely that it saved the lives of any thirsty explorers because it lives in warm areas where there is plenty of water!

24 Which oak tree made predictions?

At a place called Dodona in the Epirus region of Greece, there was a mighty oak tree, oracle of the god Zeus. Whenever a person wanted to consult the oracle – or ask a question or request of Zeus – they would write it on a piece of bronze and give it to a holy interpreter, who would communicate the request to the oak tree. The wind rustling through the branches of the sacred oak was believed to be the answer from Zeus, which was written on another sheet of bronze and given to the questioner. Some of these bronzes with questions and answers can be seen at the National Museum in Athens.

As well as the oak of Zeus (Jupiter to the Romans, Perkunas to the Slavs), laurel was sacred to the god Apollo; olive to the goddess Minerva; the lotus flower to the Hindu god Brahma and the Buddhist god Buddha. And with the flower of the holy Rosary Tree (*Melia azedarach*), people in Persia, Malaya and Singapore wove coronets to wear in their temples.

25 How did the rubber tree spread?

In order to keep the rubber tree, the Brazilian government once banned the export of seeds. But in 1876, Englishman Henry Wickam got permission to export 7000 "botanical samples" from the tree. Of these, 3000 survived. Some were planted in England and some in Ceylon (now Sri Lanka) where they flourished so that by 1930, there were 1,000,000 trees spread over 250,000 hectares of land in East Asia.

26 Who discovered the secret of silk?

A silk worm spins a thread of silk all around its body, making a cocoon in which it becomes a chrysalis and then a butterfly.

The Chinese found a way of unwinding the soft, glossy thread, which, once it was spun and woven, became the most magnificent material.

China became so famous for its silk that it was exported along the "Silk Route" to the north of the Byzantine Empire. And with the skeins of silk thread and silk fabric to sell, the trade was very profitable.

Naturally, the Chinese guarded the secret of their silk and how they used the silk-worms to obtain the thread.

But the Byzantine Emperor Justinian decided that it was worth the trouble to discover the secret.

He paid two Chinese monarchs to do this task, and they returned with cocoons hidden inside their hollow walking sticks.

It was 552 A.D. when the production of silk began in the Mediterranean.

The Arabs also produced a type of silk in Persia. About 1000 A.D. they brought the industry to Spain.

A few decades later, Ruggero, King of Sicily, introduced a way of making silk from Greece, and by the end of the 17th century, the Italian silk industry was unrivalled in Europe.

But when weavers left the main silk-making centres of Catanzaro and Genoa to begin the French silk industry, Italian silk-making declined, with French silk becoming famous all over the world.

27 What is a botanical garden?

In a botanical garden, plants are grown both for protection and to study.

This is a very old tradition. India has study documents going back 6000 years; in China, 5000 years.

And in the London, there is one of the lists of plants in the famous Hanging Gardens of Babylon at the time of King Mardukpalidd, 800 B.C.

In Europe, the Greeks and Romans kept the tradition of botanical gardens, until the Emperor Charlemagne ruled that they should be for medicinal plants. Botanical gardens run by the monasteries, however, lacked nothing.

The first botanical garden actually certified as such was the one founded by Pope Nicholas III at the Vatican in 1278, then the medical school at Salerno, Sicily, followed by the University of Prague, Cologne, Pisa, Padua, Bologne, Florence, Paris, Utrecht, Copenhagen, and, of course, the famous Royal Botanical Gardens at Kew, near London.

28 What is bio-luminescence?

Bio-luminescence is the ability of some living things to give light.

For instance, tropical seas at night shine because of an algae called *Noctiluca scintillans* (Sparkling Night-Light). In New Guinea, there is a fungus which gives out enough light to guide people quite a distance. And in Queensland, Australia, another fungus gives out a blue light which is powerful enough to read by!

There is also a moss which gets into cracks – and when it begins to sprout and grow, gives off an emerald light.

Some marcescent (rotting) wood becomes luminous in summer and autumn with fungi growing on it – this is not at all rare.

No wonder people walking through woods at night believed in elves, gnomes and fairies!

Miners will also tell of walking through underground passageways lit by beams from luminescent plants. And in any field on a moonlit summer's night, we can see the luminous wings of fireflies.

29 Which plants and animals are parasites?

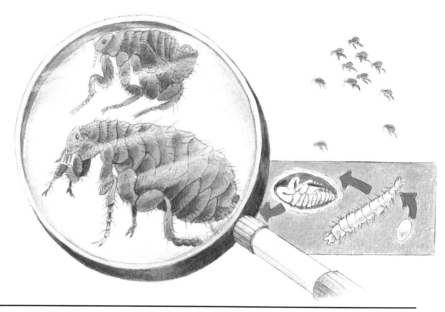

Parasites are animals and plants which live either inside or on other living things.

Sometimes this can be good, as in the case of many fungi and bacteria.

But sometimes, parasites can be dangerous, and can even cause death.

One example is the Tsetse Fly which causes the deadly sleeping sickness.

Less dangerous parasites include fleas and lice.

30 Which plants are emblems of state?

Almost all countries of the world have a plant as an emblem.
Here is a list of just a few of them.

Australia – mimosa. Greece – laurel. Canada – maple leaf. Poland – pansy. Holland – calendula. Venezuela, Argentina, Brazil and Columbia – orchid. Japan – chrysanthemum. Denmark – beech and holly. Germany and France – cornflower. Russia – sunflower. Portugal – lavender and oak. Northern Ireland – flax.

Eire – medicinal herbs. Finland – lily of the valley. Belgium – poppy. China – peony. Italy – pine tree. Finland – oak tree. England, Bulgaria, Iran, Iraq, Luxembourg, Turkey and Rumania – rose. Scotland – thistle. Wales – daffodil. Lithuania – rue. Andorra and Austria – stella alpine. Czechoslovakia – lime. Hungary – magnolia. Israel – olive.

And in the U.S.A. the violet is the most popular emblem, adopted by New Jersey, Illinois, Rhode Island and Wisconsin.

31 What is mistletoe?

This night people in Europe will see sprigs of mistletoe pinned to the doors of many homes, keeping the tradition which began with the young Druid, Ram.

Mistletoe is a semi-parasitic plant, widespread throughout most temperate and warm regions in the world. It can live on poplar trees, lime, elm, beech, nut, ash, acacia, but, of course, mainly the oak, at whose feet the young Druid fell asleep so many years ago.

Index

APRIL

Sailing

Sir Francis Drake

1 How did men sail in prehistoric times?

2 How did the Ancient Babylonians sail?

3 How did the Ancient Egyptians build their boats?

4 How was a trireme built?

5 How big were caravels?

6 How do a privateer and a pirate differ?

7 How far did the Vikings reach?

8 How was the first submersible made?

9 How does a nuclear submarine work?

10 How is it possible to survive being shipwrecked?

11 Are solo sea-crossings a recent happening?

12 How do ships enter harbour?

13 What is the use of buoys?

14 Hovercraft, seaplane, hydrofoil – what are they?

15 What is surfing?

16 What is a regatta?

17 What is an outboard motor?

18 How were sea battles once fought?

19 How is an aircraft carrier made?

20 What happens today in naval battles?

21 What made the Titanic sink?

22 How do ships float?

23 How do you sail against the wind?

24 What is a catamaran?

25 How does a compass work?

26 How can ships find their way?

27 How does an echo-sounder work?

28 How is a nautical chart made?

29 What is a container ship?

30 What is a sextant?

MAY

The Sky

An Eclipse of the Sun

1 What is a climate?

2 How do we classify climates?

3 What is a rainbow?

4 What is drought?

5 What is wind?

6 What are breezes?

7 What are seasonal and constant winds?

8 Why is the sky blue?

9 What are clouds?

10 Why does it rain?

11 What is a mist?

12 How is dew formed?

13 How do we get hail?

14 Where does snow come from?

15 What is lightning?

16 What is the ozone layer?

17 What is "The Greenhouse Effect"?

18 What is a falling star?

19 How does the moon change each month?

20 Which planets can you see with the naked eye?

21 What did ancient men see in the stars?

22 What is a comet?

23 What is the difference between planets and satellites?

24 How can we study the sky?

25 Which are the oldest types of observatories?

26 Why is the Pole Star important?

27 How is our Solar System made up?

28 What is the sun?

29 How does an eclipse of the sun happen?

30 How does an eclipse of the moon happen?

31 Which travels faster – light or sound?

JUNE

Flight

Otto and the Stork

1 Who was Icarus?

2 How do birds fly?

3 Are there birds which do not fly?

4 Which birds are the strongest fliers?

5 What problems did man face in flying?

6 What is the difference between hot air balloons and airships?

7 When were the first flying machines made?

8 When was the first true air flight?

9 How does an aeroplane fly?

10 What is a V T O L aircraft?

11 What is a variable wing-span (swing wing) aircraft?

12 Who are air traffic controllers?

13 What is the sound barrier?

14 When did Air Mail begin?

15 When was a pigeon post first used?

16 Who made the first flight across the Atlantic?

17 How does a glider fly?

18 How does a hang-glider fly?

19 When was the parachute invented?

20 Who invented the helicopter?

21 How can people fly in space?

22 What is the space shuttle?

23 Is it easy to fly a kite?

24 How does a bat fly?

25 What is a U.F.O.?

26 Are there any plants which fly?

27 Are there any fish which can fly?

28 How does flight help man?

29 Who are the flying doctors?

30 What is aerial archaeology?

JULY

Travel

Going on Holiday

1 How did people travel in prehistoric times?

2 Which were the main waterways?

3 What were the main European routes?

4 Where were the first roads built?

5 How were the Roman roads built?

6 How did the Ancient Romans travel?

7 What were the Mayan roads like?

8 What sort of roads did the Incas build?

9 Do people still use waterways for transport?

10 Who designed the canal at Corinth?

11 When was the train invented?

12 What is the Orient Express?

13 What were the first major railway tunnels?

14 What is a narrow gauge railway?

15 What is an underground system?

16 How was the Channel Tunnel built?

17 When was the car invented?

18 What are the "devil's bridges"?

19 Is motor racing only for people to watch?

20 How did ancient civilisations discover the wheel?

21 How does the electric car work?

22 When was the bicycle invented?

23 What is a cycle lane?

24 What is a mountain bike?

25 What sort of wagons did the American pioneers travel in?

26 How do people travel across snow?

27 How can dogs help in an avalanche?

28 What journey did Lewis and Clark make?

29 What is the "Check-In"?

30 What is the Duty Free shop?

31 What method of transport is the most extraordinary?

AUGUST

Science and Technology

Loading the Canoe

1 What are frozen foods?

2 How does a refrigerator work?

3 How can we keep drinks hot?

4 When were tinned foods invented?

5 How does a microwave oven work?

6 How is glass made?

7 When did metal-working begin?

8 How do sundials work?

9 How do hour glasses work?

10 When did clocks first appear?

11 Have there always been things made of rubber?

12 What are natural fibres?

13 How are artificial materials made?

14 How do we get energy from water?

15 What is an atom?

16 What is ecology?

17 What is the type of energy given off by the sun?

18 What is pollution?

19 What is meant by "biodegradable"?

20 How do we get energy from the wind?

21 Which creatures warn us of pollution?

22 How can we preserve flowers?

23 How does an electric lamp work?

24 What is biological farming?

25 What is the bar code?

26 What is a liquid crystal?

27 What types of artificial satellites are there?

28 Where does technology come to the rescue of art?

29 What type of beam is a laser beam?

30 What can we use robots for?

31 What is the difference between a computer and a calculator?

SEPTEMBER

The Human Body

My Friend Amy

1 What is the human body made of?

2 How has man changed over thousands of years?

3 What use is sport?

4 What are vitamins?

5 Why do we need to eat?

6 What is a diet?

7 How many senses do we have?

8 What is the best weight and height?

9 What happens when we are frightened?

10 What are psycho-somatic illnesses?

11 What are bio-rhythms?

12 Why do we need blood tests?

13 What is the purpose of vaccination?

14 What do white corpuscles do?

15 What is "a temperature"?

16 What are tears?

17 What is the use of X-rays?

18 What do anti-biotics do?

19 Why do we need to brush our teeth?

20 Why does the sun burn more in the mountains?

21 Is it good for us to get brown?

22 What is "mountain sickness"?

23 How do we go underwater?

24 Why do we put broken limbs in plaster?

25 What makes swimming the perfect sport?

26 Why do people need glasses?

27 What can we see if we are colour blind?

28 What is the best way to sit?

29 What is meant by something being "anatomical"?

30 What is sleep?

OCTOBER

Food and Drink

My Friend The Wolf

1 What food did prehistoric man eat?
2 When did man first begin to cook food?
3 How did prehistoric man catch the woolly mammoth?
4 How did prehistoric man catch birds?
5 How did prehistoric man catch fish?
6 Which fruit and vegetables were there in prehistoric times?
7 What animals did men first breed?
8 Where did farming begin?
9 How can we keep foods today?
10 Is coffee good or bad for you?
11 What exactly is jam?
12 What are "St. James' Shells"?
13 When was rice first grown?
14 Which types of food come from animals?
15 Which types of food do we get from vegetables?
16 When did people begin making bread?
17 When was the pizza invented?
18 Where was the hamburger invented?
19 How many types of sweeteners are there?
20 Why do we use herbs in cooking?
21 Why were spices once so precious?
22 What is yoghurt?
23 Why is milk a complete food?
24 Which plants and animals came from America?
25 When was the fork invented?
26 Is there a bread tree?
27 When did the use of tea spread?
28 What sort of food is an egg?
29 When was the cooking pot invented?
30 How did the Ancient Romans eat?
31 When did we first start eating potatoes?

NOVEMBER

Communications

The Key to a Mystery

1 Where do we get the word "bible" from?
2 Is paper an ancient product?
3 What were the first writings?
4 How do bees communicate with each other?
5 Is there a "language of flowers"?
6 How did crowns and crowning begin?
7 Why do we give orange blossom to a bride?
8 How do dogs communicate?
9 How many different calendars are there?
10 What are the Greek and Cyrillic alphabets?
11 How did our alphabet begin?
12 What were the schools like in Ancient Greece?
13 What were the schools like in Ancient Rome?
14 What about schools in the Middle Ages?
15 When did universities begin?
16 What is the Linnaeus Classification?
17 What is the story behind the laurel wreath?
18 How did printing and movable type begin?
19 What is the "mass media"?
20 What is the International Alphabet?
21 How do ships communicate?
22 What is the Morse Code?
23 What is Esperanto?
24 How many languages are spoken throughout the world?
25 Who invented the telegraph and the telephone?
26 When was the telephone invented?
27 When was television invented?
28 What is a status symbol?
29 What is the significance of the caduceus?
30 What is etiquette?

DECEMBER

Plants and Animals

The Story of Ram

1 How do flowers attract insects?
2 Why are insects important to plants?
3 What are fungi?
4 What is a Phoenix?
5 Why do plants turn towards the light?
6 When did dinosaurs live?
7 Which plants are said to be "officinal"?
8 What animals and plants are there at the Pole?
9 What is camouflage?
10 What are mosses and lichens?
11 What animals and plants are there in the desert?
12 Why are there oases in the desert?
13 Which animals are not afraid of snakes?
14 What is moulting?
15 Are gorillas dangerous?
16 Which birds live in our cities?
17 Do plants have feelings?
18 Where are the biggest trees in the world?
19 What is "symbiosis"?
20 Why do nettles sting?
21 What is the "Victoria Regia"?
22 In what ways can we use date palm trees?
23 Where does the "Travellers' Tree" grow?
24 Which oak tree made predictions?
25 How did the rubber tree spread?
26 Who discovered the secret of silk?
27 What is a botanical garden?
28 What is bio-luminescence?
29 Which plants and animals are parasites?
30 Which plants are emblems of state?
31 What is mistletoe?